THE INDEPENDENT WOMAN

Also by Simone de Beauvoir

THE INDEPENDENT WOMAN

Extracts from
The Second Sex

SIMONE DE BEAUVOIR

Translated by Constance Borde
and Sheila Malovany-Chevallier

Annotated and Introduced
by Martine Reid

VINTAGE BOOKS
A Division of Penguin Random House LLC
New York

FIRST VINTAGE BOOKS EDITION, SEPTEMBER 2018

Extracts from Le deuxième sexe *by Simone de Beauvoir*
copyright © 1949 by Éditions Gallimard, Paris
Translation copyright of extracts © 2009
by Constance Borde and Sheila Malovany-Chevallier
Translation copyright of introduction and notes © 2015
by Constance Borde and Sheila Malovany-Chevallier
This edition annotated by Martine Reid © 2008 by
Editions Gallimard, Paris

All rights reserved. Published in the United States
by Vintage Books, a division of Penguin Random
House LLC, New York, and distributed in Canada by
Random House of Canada, a division of
Penguin Random House Canada Limited, Toronto.
This translation originally published in Great Britain as
Extracts from the Second Sex by Vintage Classics, an imprint
of Penguin Random House Ltd., London, in 2015.

Vintage and colophon are registered trademarks of
Penguin Random House LLC.

This work is extracted from *Le deuxième sexe* by Simone de Beauvoir,
originally published by Editions Gallimard, Paris, in 1949. The
full-length translation of *Le deuxième sexe* was originally published
in hardcover in Great Britain as *The Second Sex* by Jonathan Cape,
a division of Penguin Random House Ltd., London, in 2009,
and subsequently published in hardcover in the United States
by Alfred A. Knopf, a division of Penguin Random House LLC,
New York, in 2010.

Introduction and annotations by Martine Reid first published in
La Femme independante by Editions Gallimard, Paris, in 2008.

The Cataloging-in-Publication data is on file
at the Library of Congress.

Vintage Books Trade Paperback ISBN: 978-0-525-56340-2
eBook ISBN: 978-0-525-56341-9

www.vintagebooks.com

Printed in the United States of America
3rd Printing

CONTENTS

EDITOR'S NOTE

From May to July 1948 the journal *Les Temps Modernes*, directed by Jean-Paul Sartre and Simone de Beauvoir, published three extracts from a "forthcoming work on the situation of woman," with the general title "Woman and Myths." They were part of the third section of the first volume of *The Second Sex* and dealt with the image that Montherlant, Claudel and Breton gave of women in their novels. Her analysis was harsh, her tone biting, and the often-virulent criticism was not long in coming. Simone de Beauvoir wrote on 3 August to the American writer Nelson Algren, with whom she was involved for a year: "[*The Second Sex*] is a big and long work that will take at least another year. I want it to be really good [. . .]. I hear it said, and this really pleases me, that the part published in *Les Temps Modernes* infuriated several men; it is a chapter devoted to the absurd myths that men cherish about women, and to the ridiculous poetry they manufacture about them. The men seem to have been hit where it hurts."

"The first volume was finished in autumn," recalled Simone de Beauvoir in *Force of Circumstance*, "and

I decided to take it right away to Gallimard. What should I call it? I thought about it for a long time with Sartre [. . .]. I thought of *The Other, The Second*: that had already been used. One evening, in my room, we spent hours throwing words around, Sartre, Bost and I. I suggested: *The Other Sex*. No. Bost proposed: *The Second Sex*, and upon reflection, it fit perfectly. I feverishly set to work on the second volume."

As of May the following year, *Les Temps Modernes* published three new extracts from the second volume: "Sexual Initiation," "The Lesbian" and "The Mother." The first two are in the part called "Formative Years" and the third in "Situation." François Mauriac, a journalist at *Le Figaro* newspaper, was particularly outraged by Simone de Beauvoir's writing on sexuality and started an inquiry into the "so-called message of Saint-Germain-des-Prés" and expected "young intellectuals and writers" to totally disavow the surrealist and existentialist movements whose influence he claimed to see in Simone de Beauvoir's work. Reactions were not long in coming and the Catholic writer, probably to his great surprise, did not find the unanimous condemnation he was expecting. Authors brought quite nuanced answers to the question that rather proved, with all due respect to Mauriac, that an inevitable evolution was occurring in postwar France, an evolution in morals and mentalities and in men's and women's relations.

In June 1949 the first volume of *Le Deuxième Sexe* (*The Second Sex*), subtitled "Les Faits et les mythes"

("Facts and Myths"), was published by Gallimard (with the author's name in black capital letters on an ivory cover, and the title in red capitals). It carried a strip embellished with a picture of Simone de Beauvoir and Jean-Paul Sartre at the Café Flore, with the caption "Woman, this unknown." The book was dedicated to Jacques Bost, and the dedication was followed by quotations from Pythagoras and Poullain de la Barre, one of the first, in the seventeenth century, to have defended the equality of the sexes. Twenty-two thousand copies were sold in the first week, while reviewers went wild.

In August *Paris-Match* published extracts from the second volume in its issues of 6 and 13 August: "A woman calls women to freedom," the weekly proclaims. This volume, subtitled "Lived Experience," came out in November. It carried two quotations as epigraphs, one by Kierkegaard and the other by Sartre. "One is not born, but rather becomes, woman" can be read in the first lines of the first chapter. "No biological, psychical or economic destiny defines the figure that the human female takes on in society; it is civilization as a whole that elaborates this intermediary product between the male and the eunuch that is called feminine." From then on, it was no longer a question of simply mentioning facts and analyzing a few forms of literary mythification, but of striking at the heart of the edifice of collective representations. Repeated then thousands of times, in all languages, the phrase served as the keystone of feminist thinking for the second half of the twentieth century, and what it says belongs to a veritable conceptual revolution.

In 1949 Simone de Beauvoir was forty-one years old. One word encapsulates her existence up to that point and for a long time afterward: freedom. In her autobiographical opus in which, starting in the 1960s, she resuscitated the past with rare openness, the notion was felt, as of adolescence, as a profound and irrepressible drive. Superficially, the destiny of a girl of the Parisian bourgeoisie in the 1920s seemed all worked out: marriage and motherhood will "raise" her to the rank of wife and then mother; society doesn't expect anything else of her. If by chance she is educated, if she likes studying enough to want a profession, she'll feel very quickly that there are necessary sacrifices: she will give up her career plans to devote herself entirely to her family. That is what Colette Yver's novels, which Beauvoir's father liked so much, taught; and that is what the adolescent firmly rejected. She will not be a "housewife," she will be mistress of her own life. The struggle was first of all on an individual level. Exist for oneself, break with existing patterns, be free to dispose of one's own life. How? By acquiring a financial and intellectual autonomy, by studying to be able to have a real profession. Simone de Beauvoir counted on becoming free through her own capacities, and not without difficulty. In her family, as in thousands of others, everything was a question of powerful prejudices and harsh discussions: the books one could read, the friends one could see, the young men with whom one was allowed to go out, the studies that could be envisaged. The adolescent stood fast (without having total control), decided she would be a teacher (a feminine profession) and then that she would sit for the philosophy *agrégation* (a far more daring gesture).

Once she acquired her intellectual autonomy (by getting her philosophy *agrégation*), and once she was in possession of a profession, and thus a salary, Simone de Beauvoir had to acquire real independence in the sentimental area. It was harder than it seemed. It is fine to be a bluestocking (after all, the phenomenon had been going on for at least a whole century), but a liberated bluestocking! With Jean-Paul Sartre, whom she met in January 1929, the "contract" guaranteeing each other's freedom was set up rather easily: it was understood that the affection that united them was "necessary," but it did not exclude "contingent" loves, on either side. Marriage and even living together (the household chores would quickly risk creating some dependence) were out of the question; motherhood even more so: a project, the only one that was worth it, from an intellectual and existential point of view, was spelled out. "Two concerns dominated [my youth]," wrote Simone de Beauvoir in *The Prime of Life*, "to live and fulfill my still abstract vocation as a writer, that is to find the point of entry of literature in my life."

At this stage, her lucidity was remarkable, and her determination as well: however, Simone de Beauvoir had still only worked for herself. She didn't conceal this in her autobiography: she is not very interested in politics; history is no concern of hers; her "social" conscience consists of lip-service solidarity with those who deal with a just cause. "As of 1939, everything changed." All of a sudden, history imposed its brutal presence; political choices were no longer vain words; the practice of literature became a veritable necessity. "Literature appears when something in life goes out of whack," she says in *The Prime of Life*; "the first condition in order to write [. . .] is for reality to cease being taken for granted. Only then is one able to see it and to present it to be seen." That was not the only obvious change. While the circle of people that she saw grew, the feeling of a "condition" common to women, of whom she was a part and who most often profited from it as much as they suffered from it, became clearer. "On many points, I realized how much, before the war, I had sinned by abstraction [. . .]; I hadn't realized that there was a feminine condition," she admitted.

The war and the early 1940s were a crucial period for Simone de Beauvoir: it marked her passage from concerns about individual liberty to a consciousness raised within a collective perspective; it precipitated her entry into a literature situated between philosophical essay and fiction, a desire to write about herself, and original formal research. Sartre's companion continued, with him, to seek her way. Her literary beginnings were clearly marked more by experimental attempts than by real successes. The writer's modesty, the sharp critical sense that stayed with her forever, would cause her to later judge (too) harshly this first period of her work when, in the footsteps of Virginia Woolf but also the great American novelists, Hemingway, Melville and Faulkner, she tried to describe the world from the subjective point of view of the character. The collection of short stories, *When Things of the Spirit Come First (Anne, ou quand prime le spiritual)*, could not find a publisher; her second novel, *She Came to Stay (L'Invitée)*, of a philosophical nature, met with real success in 1943; a metaphysical and political reflection on the Resistance, *The Blood of Others (Le Sang des autres)*, had no more than critical success, as did *All Men are Mortal (Tous les hommes sont mortels)*. Just after the war, prodded by Sartre, Simone de Beauvoir tried out the theater with *The Useless Mouths (Les Bouches inutiles)*, but the play was a flop. After two essays, *Pyrrhus and Cinéas* and *The Ethics of Ambiguity (Pour une morale de l'ambiguité)*, the account of her trip to America, published in 1948, was, on the other hand, well received by the public.

In the meantime, beginning in 1946, Simone de Beauvoir began thinking about a book on this "feminine condition," a condition that she had become brutally aware of and, moved by a sense of urgency, wanted to write about. The domination of man over woman, pervasive everywhere, needed to be analyzed and criticized, and the subject brought into the open wherever it showed itself, thought out in all its forms, and from all points of view. Biology, history, philosophy, politics and anthropology are all convened to put this domination on trial, and even more so as its relevance to the situation of workers, or that of black Americans, becomes obvious—the comparison will come up again and again. From this perspective, the issue would be to understand what was happening and then to galvanize change; this would mean analyzing the motives and circumstances of the dependence, before calling for independence. "The Independent Woman" is the title of the last chapter that we have chosen to reproduce, and it is no surprise: *The Second Sex* is (also) a true lesson in liberty, given by a liberated woman, as free in body and spirit as a specific period allowed, and as a consciousness engaged in a process of active criticism regarding her time permitted.

Some books come at the right moment: they constitute a rash of ideas of their time, while opening up totally new perspectives; they give name to what is commonly shared, but they call for their examination and then going beyond that; their authors render precise observations, but they are equally capable of creating the conceptual tools that will serve to criticize what they have observed. *The Second Sex* is one of these books. Everything in Simone de Beauvoir's approach evoked above—her daring and determined itinerary—lead, as if naturally, to this result: "[. . .] wanting to talk about myself, I decided that I had to describe the feminine condition. [. . .] I tried to put some logic in the picture, incoherent at first sight, that was in front of me: in any case, the man posited himself as Subject and considered the woman as an object, as the Other. [. . .] I set out to take a look at women, and I went from surprise to surprise. It's strange and stimulating to suddenly discover, at the age of forty, an aspect of the world so obvious, but that no one ever saw."

Simone de Beauvoir, as a philosopher, formulated the relation that has structured the relationship between man and woman for millennia: the man sees, the woman is seen; man is subject, woman is object, *other, second,* irremediably so; man is culture, woman is nature, prisoner of her physiological condition, of this womb that subjects her to her destiny, maternity. Undoubtedly, all through history with an astonishing stubbornness, women's voices have been raised to protest at this condition that her domination created, but also to claim civil and political rights. Women authors in particular, under attack from the literary milieu, took care to question the relations between men and women in their novels when they were not calling for equality in articles, pamphlets and essays. Marie de Gournay, Olympe de Gouges, Mme de Genlis and George Sand were among them, and were supported in their claims by a Poullain de la Barre, a Condorcet or a Saint-Simon. Yet it is not this proto-feminist history that interests Simone de Beauvoir, or even the social and political claims that marked the first half of the twentieth century. The radicalness of her position rests upon an existentialist conviction: existence precedes essence; in this perspective, there is no feminine "nature" and referring to some kind of feminine "essence" makes no sense. Criticism of existing discourses (biology, psychoanalysis, historical materialism); criticism of history that shows that "men have always held all the concrete powers"; criticism of literary representations (these famous "myths" conveying contradictory images, mummy and whore, saint and bitch, sublime woman and damned woman); criticism of the "ages" of the woman, beginning with childhood, adolescence and her sexual initiation; criticism of adopted attitudes in which she alienates herself (narcissism, love, mysticism); ultimately a call for emancipation and independence, accompanied by the wish to see reign one day not an equality in difference—too easy an alibi, a refrain from another age—but a true, ontological equality constitute the remarkable steps of a perfectly new book, animated by resolutely anti-naturalistic thinking.

The strength of *The Second Sex* consists in denouncing the sociohistorical character connected to the notion of "woman" (from this perspective, she announces the notion of "gender," as Françoise Héritier reminds us) and in freeing it from being reduced to any supposed nature. The originality of the book lies in its ambition to examine the human sciences as well as literature, then to make "becoming woman," from childhood to old age, an object of reflection in its own right, in a perspective borrowed from phenomenology. The courage of such a work, in which the author involved herself *in person* (which did not fail to shock), rests on the fact that Beauvoir did not hesitate to apply to women themselves, "half victim, half accomplice," as the quote from Sartre in the epigraph to the second volume says, the critical eye that was applied elsewhere—that is, to denounce the connivance that links them willingly to the one who dominates them. It is understandable that *The Second Sex* might have (greatly) irritated readers on the right as on the left, both men and women. Without doubt, some sixty years later, it bears the mark of its time: in particular, it reaches the limits of the philosophy that underpins it, as well as the political thinking that nourishes it. For all that, its seminal character cannot be diminished, nor its formidable influence be denied. As soon as it appeared, it was translated into several dozen languages; in the United States, Betty Friedan made it the spearhead in the feminist combat for equality and parity, and this goes for nearly every country in Europe, followed by Latin America and Asia. Moreover, Simone de Beauvoir herself modified some of her views somewhat, first by abandoning the idea of a purely political revolution in favor of a specifically female combat for the improvement of their condition (here is where she *becomes* feminist, as she would explain later on), then by criticizing her own analyses as being not materialist enough in her eyes, but nonetheless without reneging on her original thesis.

The Second Sex so continuously and deeply impregnated the thinking about the feminine, and feminism, from 1949 on that upon rereading it one is often surprised by the resistance that it has encountered. The ideas it defended have become realities, have advanced into our thinking and have, to a certain point, been accomplished. On the death of Simone de Beauvoir in 1986, Elisabeth Badinter dedicated an article to her in *Le Nouvel Observateur.* Entitled "Women of France, you owe her everything!," it recalled the intellectual impact of one of the most important texts of the second half of the twentieth century. French women, assuredly, owe her many things, but they are not the only ones: thanks to Simone de Beauvoir, the notorious "feminine condition," universally shared, has been changed forever.

Martine Reid, 2008
For Gisèle Halimi

NOTE ON THE TEXT

Published by Gallimard in 1949, *The Second Sex* comprises two volumes and a total of 800 pages. We have chosen to reproduce the introduction to the first volume (pp. 3–17), as well as chapter 14, "The Independent Woman" (pp. 737–68), and the final pages of the second volume (pp. 769–82). (All page numbers refer to the full-length 2009 Vintage Classics edition.) The author's notes are indicated by asterisks; the editor's notes are indicated by numbers collected at the end of the book.

I would like to thank Sylvie Le Bon de Beauvoir for her permission to reproduce this work and for rereading the notes that accompany it.

THE INDEPENDENT WOMAN

INTRODUCTION

I hesitated a long time before writing a book on woman. The subject is irritating, especially for women; and it is not new. Enough ink has flowed over the quarrel about feminism; it is now almost over: let's not talk about it anymore. Yet it is still being talked about. And the volumes of idiocies churned out over this past century do not seem to have clarified the problem. Besides, is there a problem? And what is it? Are there even women? True, the theory of the eternal feminine still has its followers, they whisper, "Even in Russia, *women* are still very much women"; but other well-informed people—and also at times those same ones—lament, "Woman is losing herself, woman is lost." It is hard to know any longer if women still exist, if they will always exist, if there should be women at all, what place they hold in this world, what place they should hold. "Where are the women?" asked a short-lived magazine recently.[*] But first, what is a woman? "*Tota mulier in utero*: she is a womb," some say. Yet speaking of certain women, the

---

[*] Out of print today, entitled *Franchise*.

experts proclaim, "They are not women," even though they have a uterus like the others. Everyone agrees there are females in the human species; today, as in the past, they make up about half of humanity; and yet we are told that "femininity is in jeopardy"; we are urged, "Be women, stay women, become women." So not every female human being is necessarily a woman; she must take part in this mysterious and endangered reality known as femininity. Is femininity secreted by the ovaries? Is it enshrined in a Platonic heaven? Is a frilly petticoat enough to bring it down to earth? Although some women zealously strive to embody it, the model has never been patented. It is typically described in vague and shimmering terms borrowed from a clairvoyant's vocabulary. In St. Thomas's time it was an essence defined with as much certainty as the sedative quality of a poppy. But conceptualism has lost ground: biological and social sciences no longer believe there are immutably determined entities that define given characteristics like those of the woman, the Jew or the black; science considers characteristics as secondary reactions to a *situation*. If there is no such thing today as femininity, it is because there never was. Does the word "woman," then, have no content? It is what advocates of Enlightenment philosophy, rationalism or nominalism vigorously assert: women are, among human beings, merely those who are arbitrarily designated by the word "woman"; American women in particular are inclined to think that woman as such no longer exists. If some backward individual still takes herself for a woman, her friends advise her to undergo psychoanalysis to get rid of this obsession. Referring to a book—a very irritating one at that—*Modern Woman: The Lost Sex*, Dorothy Parker[1] wrote: "I cannot be fair about books that treat women as women. My idea is that all of us, men as well as women, whoever we are, should be considered as human beings." But nominalism is a doctrine that falls a bit short; and it is easy for antifeminists to show that women *are* not men. Certainly woman like man is a human being; but such an assertion is abstract; the fact is that every concrete human being is always uniquely situated. Rejecting the notions of the eternal feminine, the black soul or the Jewish character is not to deny that there are today Jews, blacks or women: this denial is not a liberation for those concerned, but an inauthentic flight. Clearly, no woman can claim without bad faith to be situated beyond her sex. A few years ago, a well-known woman[2] writer refused to have her portrait appear in a series of photographs devoted specifically to women writers. She wanted to be included in the men's category; but to get this privilege, she used her husband's influence. Women who assert they are men still claim masculine consideration and respect. I also remember a young Trotskyite standing on a platform during a stormy meeting, about to come to blows in spite of her obvious fragility. She was denying her feminine frailty; but it was for the love of a militant man she wanted to be equal to. The defiant position that American women

5

occupy proves they are haunted by the feeling of their own femininity. And the truth is that anyone can clearly see that humanity is split into two categories of individuals with manifestly different clothes, faces, bodies, smiles, movements, interests and occupations; these differences are perhaps superficial; perhaps they are destined to disappear. What is certain is that for the moment they exist in a strikingly obvious way.

If the female function is not enough to define woman, and if we also reject the explanation of the "eternal feminine," but if we accept, even temporarily, that there are women on the earth, we then have to ask: what is a woman?

Merely stating the problem suggests an immediate answer to me. It is significant that I pose it. It would never occur to a man to write a book on the singular situation of males in humanity.* If I want to define myself, I first have to say, "I am a woman"; all other assertions will arise from this basic truth. A man never begins by positing himself as an individual of a certain sex: that he is a man is obvious. The categories "masculine" and "feminine" appear as symmetrical in a formal way on town hall records or identification papers. The relation of the two sexes is not that of two electrical poles: the man represents both the positive and the neuter to such an extent

* The Kinsey Report,[3] for example, confines itself to defining the sexual characteristics of the American man, which is completely different.

that in French *hommes* designates human beings, the particular meaning of the word *vir* being assimilated into the general meaning of the word "homo." Woman is the negative, to such a point that any determination is imputed to her as a limitation, without reciprocity. I used to get annoyed in abstract discussions to hear men tell me: "You think such and such a thing because you're a woman." But I know my only defense is to answer, "I think it because it is true," thereby eliminating my subjectivity; it was out of the question to answer, "And you think the contrary because you are a man," because it is understood that being a man is not a particularity; a man is in his right by virtue of being man; it is the woman who is in the wrong. In fact, just as for the ancients there was an absolute vertical that defined the oblique, there is an absolute human type that is masculine. Woman has ovaries and a uterus; such are the particular conditions that lock her in her subjectivity; some even say she thinks with her hormones. Man vainly forgets that his anatomy also includes hormones and testicles. He grasps his body as a direct and normal link with the world that he believes he apprehends in all objectivity, whereas he considers woman's body an obstacle, a prison, burdened by everything that particularizes it. "The female is female by virtue of a certain *lack* of qualities," Aristotle said. "We should regard women's nature as suffering from natural defectiveness." And St. Thomas in his turn decreed that woman was an "incomplete man," an "incidental" being. This is what the Genesis story symbolizes, where Eve appears as if drawn from Adam's "supernumerary" bone, in Bossuet's words. Humanity is male, and man defines woman, not in herself, but in relation to himself; she is not considered an autonomous being. "Woman, the relative being," writes Michelet. Thus Monsieur Benda declares in *Uriel's Report*:[4] "A man's body has meaning by itself, disregarding the body of the woman, whereas the woman's body seems devoid of meaning without reference to the male. Man thinks himself without woman. Woman does not think herself without man." And she is nothing other than what man decides; she is thus called "the sex," meaning that the male sees her essentially as a sexed being; for him she is sex, so she is it in the absolute. She determines and differentiates herself in relation to man, and he does not in relation to her; she is the inessential in front of the essential. He is the Subject; he is the Absolute. She is the Other.*

---

* This idea has been expressed in its most explicit form by E. Levinas in his essay on *Time and the Other*.[5] He expresses it like this: "Is there not a situation where alterity would be borne by a being in a positive sense, as essence? What is the alterity that does not purely and simply enter into the opposition of two species of the same genus? I think that the absolutely contrary contrary, whose contrariety is in no way affected by the relationship that can be established between it and its correlative, the contrariety that permits its terms to remain absolutely other, is the feminine. Sex is not some specific difference . . . Neither is the difference between the sexes a contradiction . . . Neither is the difference between the sexes the duality

8

The category of *Other* is as original as consciousness itself. The duality between Self and Other can be found in the most primitive societies, in the most ancient mythologies; this division did not always fall into the category of the division of the sexes, it was not based on any empirical given: this comes out in works like Granet's on Chinese thought,[6] and Dumézil's on India and Rome.[7] In couples such as Varuna-Mitra, Uranos-Zeus, Sun-Moon, Day-Night, no feminine element is involved at the outset; neither in Good-Evil, auspicious and inauspicious, left and right, God and Lucifer; alterity is the fundamental category of human thought. No group ever defines itself as One without immediately setting up the Other opposite itself. It only takes three travelers brought together by chance in the same train compartment for the rest of the travelers to become vaguely hostile "others." Village people view anyone not belonging to the village as suspicious "others." For the native of a country, inhabitants of other countries are viewed as "foreigners"; Jews are the "others" for anti-Semites, blacks

of two complementary terms, for two complementary terms presuppose a preexisting whole . . . [A]lterity is accomplished in the feminine. The term is on the same level as, but in meaning opposed to, consciousness," I suppose Mr. Levinas is not forgetting that woman also is consciousness for herself. But it is striking that he deliberately adopts a man's point of view, disregarding the reciprocity of the subject and the object. When he writes that woman is mystery, he assumes that she is mystery for man. So this apparently objective description, is in fact an affirmation of masculine privilege.

for racist Americans, indigenous people for colonists, proletarians for the propertied classes. After studying the diverse forms of primitive society in depth, Lévi-Strauss could conclude: "The passage from the state of Nature to the state of Culture is defined by man's ability to think biological relations as systems of oppositions; duality, alternation, opposition, and symmetry, whether occurring in defined or less clear form, are not so much phenomena to explain as fundamental and immediate givens of social reality."* These phenomena could not be understood if human reality were solely a *Mitsein*[9] based on solidarity and friendship. On the contrary, they become clear if, following Hegel, a fundamental hostility to any other consciousness is found in consciousness itself; the subject posits itself only in opposition; it asserts itself as the essential and sets up the other as inessential, as the object.

But the other consciousness has an opposing reciprocal claim: traveling, a local is shocked to realize that in neighboring countries locals view him as a foreigner; between villages, clans, nations and classes there are wars, potlatches, agreements, treaties and struggles that remove the absolute meaning from the idea of the Other and bring out its relativity; whether one likes it or not, individuals and groups have no choice but to recognize the reciprocity of their relation. How

---

* See Claude Lévi-Strauss, *The Elementary Structures of Kinship*. I thank Claude Lévi-Strauss for sharing the proofs of his thesis that I drew on heavily, particularly in the second part, pp. 78-92.[8]

is it, then, that between the sexes this reciprocity has not been put forward, that one of the terms has been asserted as the only essential one, denying any relativity in regard to its correlative, defining the latter as pure alterity? Why do women not contest male sovereignty? No subject posits itself spontaneously and at once as the inessential from the outset; it is not the Other who, defining itself as Other, defines the One; the Other is posited as Other by the One positing itself as One. But in order for the Other not to turn into the One, the Other has to submit to this foreign point of view. Where does this submission in woman come from?

There are other cases where, for a shorter or longer time, one category has managed to dominate another absolutely. It is often numerical inequality that confers this privilege: the majority imposes its law on or persecutes the minority. But women are not a minority like American blacks, or like Jews: there are as many women as men on the earth. Often, the two opposing groups concerned were once independent of each other; either they were not aware of each other in the past or they accepted each other's autonomy; and some historical event subordinated the weaker to the stronger: the Jewish diaspora, slavery in America, or the colonial conquests are facts with dates. In these cases, for the oppressed there was a *before*: they share a past, a tradition, sometimes a religion, or a culture. In this sense, the parallel Bebel draws between women and the proletariat[10] would be the best founded: pro-

11

letarians are not a numerical minority either and yet they have never formed a separate group. However, not *one* event but a whole historical development explains their existence as a class and accounts for the distribution of *these* individuals in this class. There have not always been proletarians: there have always been women; they are women by their physiological structure; as far back as history can be traced, they have always been subordinate to men; their dependence is not the consequence of an event or a becoming, it did not *happen*. Alterity here appears to be an absolute, partly because it falls outside the accidental nature of historical fact. A situation created over time can come undone at another time—blacks in Haiti for one are a good example; on the contrary, a natural condition seems to defy change. In truth, nature is no more an immutable given than is historical reality. If woman discovers herself as the inessential, and never turns into the essential, it is because she does not bring about this transformation herself. Proletarians say "we." So do blacks. Positing themselves as subjects, they thus transform the bourgeois or whites into "others." Women—except in certain abstract gatherings such as conferences—do not use "we"; men say "women" and women adopt this word to refer to themselves; but they do not posit themselves authentically as Subjects. The proletarians made the revolution in Russia, the blacks in Haiti, the Indo-Chinese are fighting in Indochina. Women's actions have never been more than symbolic agitation; they have won only what men have been willing to concede to them; they have taken nothing; they have received. It is that they lack the concrete means to organize themselves into a unit that could posit itself in opposition. They have no past, no history, no religion of their own; and unlike the proletariat, they have no solidarity of labor or interests; they even lack their own space that makes communities of American blacks, or the Jews in ghettos, or the workers in Saint-Denis or Renault factories. They live dispersed among men, tied by homes, work, economic interests and social conditions to certain men—fathers or husbands—more closely than to other women. As bourgeois women, they are in solidarity with bourgeois men and not with women proletarians; as white women, they are in solidarity with white men and not with black women. The proletariat could plan to massacre the whole ruling class; a fanatic Jew or black could dream of seizing the secret of the atomic bomb and turning all of humanity entirely Jewish or entirely black: but a woman could not even dream of exterminating males. The tie that binds her to her oppressors is unlike any other. The division of the sexes is a biological given, not a moment in human history. Their opposition took shape within an original *Mitsein* and she has not broken it. The couple is a fundamental unit with the two halves riveted to each other: cleavage of society by sex is not possible. This is the fundamental characteristic of woman: she is the Other at the heart of a whole whose two components are necessary to each other.

One might think that this reciprocity would have facilitated her liberation; when Hercules spins wool at Omphale's feet, his desire enchains him. Why was Omphale unable to acquire long-lasting power? Medea, in revenge against Jason, kills her children: this brutal legend suggests that the bond attaching the woman to her child could have given her a formidable upper hand. In *Lysistrata*, Aristophanes lightheartedly imagined a group of women who, uniting together for the social good, tried to take advantage of men's need for them: but it is only a comedy. The legend that claims that the ravished Sabine women resisted their ravishers with obstinate sterility also recounts that by whipping them with leather straps, the men magically won them over into submission. Biological need—sexual desire and desire for posterity—which makes the male dependent on the female, has not liberated women socially. Master and slave are also linked by a reciprocal economic need that does not free the slave. That is, in the master-slave relation, the master does not *posit* the need he has for the other; he holds the power to satisfy this need and does not mediate it; the slave, on the other hand, out of dependence, hope or fear, internalizes his need for the master; however equally compelling the need may be to them both, it always plays in favor of the oppressor over the oppressed: this explains the slow pace of working-class liberation, for example. Now woman has always been, if not man's slave, at least his vassal; the two sexes have never divided the world up equally;

and still today, even though her condition is changing, woman is heavily handicapped. In no country is her legal status identical to man's, and often it puts her at a considerable disadvantage. Even when her rights are recognized abstractly, long-standing habit keeps them from being concretely manifested in customs. Economically, men and women almost form two castes; all things being equal, the former have better jobs, higher wages and greater chances to succeed than their new female competitors; they occupy many more places in industry, in politics, and so on, and they hold the most important positions. In addition to their concrete power they are invested with a prestige whose tradition is reinforced by the child's whole education: the present incorporates the past, and in the past all history was made by males. At the moment that women are beginning to share in the making of the world, this world still belongs to men: men have no doubt about this, and women barely doubt it. Refusing to be the Other, refusing complicity with man, would mean renouncing all the advantages an alliance with the superior caste confers on them. Lord-man will materially protect liege-woman and will be in charge of justifying her existence: along with the economic risk, she eludes the metaphysical risk of a freedom that must invent its goals without help. Indeed, beside every individual's claim to assert himself as subject—an ethical claim—lies the temptation to flee freedom and to make himself into a thing: it is a pernicious path because the individual, passive, alienated and lost, is prey to a foreign will, cut off from his transcendence, robbed of all worth. But it is an easy path: the anguish and stress of authentically assumed existence are thus avoided. The man who sets the woman up as an *Other* will thus find in her a deep complicity. Hence woman makes no claim for herself as subject because she lacks the concrete means, because she senses the necessary link connecting her to man without positing its reciprocity, and because she often derives satisfaction from her role as *Other*.

But a question immediately arises: how did this whole story begin? It is understandable that the duality of the sexes, like all duality, be expressed in conflict. It is understandable that if one of the two succeeded in imposing its superiority, it had to establish itself as absolute. It remains to be explained how it was that man won at the outset. It seems possible that women might have carried off the victory, or that the battle might never be resolved. Why is it that this world has always belonged to men and that only today things are beginning to change? Is this change a good thing? Will it bring about an equal sharing of the world between men and women or not?

These questions are far from new; they have already had many answers; but the very fact that woman is *Other* challenges all the justifications that men have ever given: these were only too clearly dictated by their own interest. "Everything that men have written about women should be viewed with suspicion, because they are both judge and party," wrote Poulain de la

Barre,[11] a little-known seventeenth-century feminist. Males have always and everywhere paraded their satisfaction of feeling they are kings of creation. "Blessed be the Lord our God, and the Lord of all worlds that has not made me a woman," Jews say in their morning prayers; meanwhile their wives resignedly murmur: "Blessed be the Lord for creating me according to His will." Among the blessings Plato thanked the gods for was, first, being born free and not a slave, and second, a man and not a woman. But males could not have enjoyed this privilege so fully had they not considered it as founded in the absolute and in eternity: they sought to make the fact of their supremacy a right. "Those who made and compiled the laws, being men, favored their own sex, and the jurisconsults have turned the laws into principles," Poulain de la Barre continues. Lawmakers, priests, philosophers, writers and scholars have gone to great lengths to prove that women's subordinate condition was willed in heaven and profitable on earth. Religions forged by men reflect this will for domination: they found ammunition in the legends of Eve and Pandora. They have put philosophy and theology in their service, as seen in the previously cited words of Aristotle and St. Thomas. Since ancient times, satirists and moralists have delighted in depicting women's weaknesses. The violent indictments brought against them all through French literature are well-known: Montherlant,[12] with less verve, picks up the tradition from Jean de Meung. This hostility seems sometimes founded but is often gratuitous; in truth, it covers up a more or less skillfully camouflaged will to self-justification. "It is much easier to accuse one sex than to excuse the other," says Montaigne.[13] In certain cases, the process is transparent. It is striking, for example, that the Roman code limiting a wife's rights invokes "the imbecility and fragility of the sex" just when a weakening family structure makes her a threat to male heirs. It is striking that in the sixteenth century, to keep a married woman under wardship, the authority of St. Augustine affirming "the wife is an animal neither reliable nor stable" is called on, whereas the unmarried woman is recognized as capable of managing her own affairs. Montaigne well understood the arbitrariness and injustice of the lot assigned to women: "Women are not wrong at all when they reject the rules of life that have been introduced into the world, inasmuch as it is the men who have made these without them. There is a natural plotting and scheming between them and us." But he does not go so far as to champion their cause. It is only in the eighteenth century that deeply democratic men begin to consider the issue objectively. Diderot,[15] for one, tries to prove that, like man, woman is a human being. A bit later, John Stuart Mill[16] ardently defends women. But these philosophers are exceptional in their impartiality. In the nineteenth century the feminist quarrel[17] once again becomes a partisan quarrel; one of the consequences of the Industrial Revolution is that women enter the labor force: at that point, women's demands leave the realm of the theoretical and find economic grounds; their adversaries become all the more aggressive; even though landed property is partially discredited, the bourgeoisie clings to the old values where family solidity guarantees private property: it insists all the more fiercely that woman's place should be in the home as her emancipation becomes a real threat; even within the working class, men tried to thwart women's liberation because women were becoming dangerous competitors—especially as women were used to working for low salaries. To prove women's inferiority, antifeminists began to draw not only, as before, on religion, philosophy and theology, but also on science: biology, experimental psychology, and so forth. At most they were willing to grant "separate but equal status" to the *other* sex. That winning formula is most significant: it is exactly that formula the Jim Crow laws[18] put into practice with regard to black Americans; this so-called egalitarian segregation served only to introduce the most extreme forms of discrimination. This convergence is in no way pure chance: whether it is race, caste, class or sex reduced to an inferior condition, the justification process is the same. "The eternal feminine" corresponds to "the black soul" or "the Jewish character." However, the Jewish problem[19] on the whole is very different from the two others: for the anti-Semite, the Jew is more an enemy than an inferior and no place on this earth is recognized as his own; it would be preferable to see him annihilated. But there are deep analogies between the situations of women and blacks: both are liberated today from the same paternalism, and the former master caste wants to keep them "in their place," that is, the place chosen for them; in both cases, they praise, more or less sincerely, the virtues of the "good black," the carefree, childlike, merry soul of the resigned black, and the woman who is a "true woman"—frivolous, infantile, irresponsible, the woman subjugated to man. In both cases, the ruling caste bases its argument on the state of affairs it created itself. The familiar line from George Bernard Shaw[20] sums it up: "The white American relegates the black to the rank of shoe-shine boy, and then concludes that blacks are only good for shining shoes." The same vicious circle can be found in all analogous circumstances: when an individual or a group of individuals is kept in a situation of inferiority, the fact is that he or they *are* inferior. But the scope of the verb *to be* must be understood; bad faith means giving it a substantive value, when in fact it has the sense of the Hegelian dynamic: *to be* is to have become, to have been made as one manifests oneself. Yes, women in general *are* today inferior to men; that is, their situation provides them with fewer possibilities: the question is whether this state of affairs must be perpetuated.

Many men wish it would be: not all men have yet laid down their arms. The conservative bourgeoisie continues to view women's liberation as a danger threatening their morality and their interests.

Some men feel threatened by women's competition. In *Hebdo-Latin*[21] the other day, a student declared: "Every woman student who takes a position as a doctor or lawyer is *stealing* a place from us." That student never questioned his rights over this world. Economic interests are not the only ones in play. One of the benefits that oppression secures for the oppressor is that the humblest among them feels *superior*: in the United States, a "poor white" from the South can console himself for not being a "dirty nigger"; and more prosperous whites cleverly exploit this pride. Likewise, the most mediocre of males believes himself a demigod next to women. It was easier for M. de Montherlant to think himself a hero in front of women (handpicked, by the way) than to act the man among men, a role that many women assumed better than he did. Thus, in one of his articles in *Le Figaro Littéraire* in September 1948, M. Claude Mauriac[22]— whom everyone admires for his powerful originality— could* write about women. "*We* listen in a tone [sic!] of polite indifference . . . to the most brilliant one among them, knowing that her intelligence, in a more or less dazzling way, reflects ideas that come from *us*." Clearly his female interlocutor does not reflect M. Mauriac's own ideas, since he is known not to have any; that she reflects ideas originating with men is possible: among males themselves, more than one of them takes as

---

* At least he thought he could.

his own opinions he did not invent; one might wonder if it would not be in M. Claude Mauriac's interest to converse with a good reflection of Descartes, Marx or Gide rather than with himself; what is remarkable is that with the ambiguous "we," he identifies with St. Paul, Hegel, Lenin and Nietzsche, and from their heights he looks down on the herd of women who dare to speak to him on an equal footing; frankly, I know of more than one woman who would not put up with M. Mauriac's "tone of polite indifference."

I have stressed this example because of its disarming masculine naïveté. Men profit in many other more subtle ways from woman's alterity. For all those suffering from an inferiority complex, this is a miraculous liniment; no one is more arrogant toward women, more aggressive or more disdainful, than a man anxious about his own virility. Those who are not threatened by their fellow men are far more likely to recognize woman as a counterpart; but even for them the myth of the Woman, of the Other, remains precious for many reasons;[*] they can hardly be blamed for

---

[*] The article by Michel Carrouges on this theme in *Cahiers du Sud*, no. 292, is significant.[23] He writes with indignation: "if only there were no feminine myth but only bands of cooks, matrons, prostitutes and bluestockings with functions of pleasure or utility!" So, according to him, woman has no existence for herself; he only takes into account her *function* in the male world. Her finality is in man; in fact, it is possible to prefer her poetic "function" to all others. The exact question is why she should be defined in relation to the man.

not wanting to lightheartedly sacrifice all the benefits they derive from the myth: they know what they lose by relinquishing the woman of their dreams, but they do not know what the woman of tomorrow will bring them. It takes great abnegation to refuse to posit oneself as unique and absolute Subject. Besides, the vast majority of men do not explicitly make this position their own. They do not *posit* woman as inferior: they are too imbued today with the democratic ideal not to recognize all human beings as equals. Within the family, the male child and then the young man sees the woman as having the same social dignity as the adult male; afterward, he experiences in desire and love the resistance and independence of the desired and loved woman; married, he respects in his wife the spouse and the mother, and in the concrete experience of married life she affirms herself opposite him as a freedom. He can thus convince himself that there is no longer a social hierarchy between the sexes and that on the whole, in spite of their differences, woman is an equal. As he nevertheless recognizes some points of inferiority—professional incapacity being the predominant one—he attributes them to nature. When he has an attitude of benevolence and partnership toward a woman, he applies the principle of abstract equality; and he does not *posit* the concrete inequality he recognizes. But as soon as he clashes with her, the situation is reversed. He will apply the concrete inequality theme and will even allow himself to disavow abstract equality.* This is how many men affirm, with quasi-good faith, that women are equal to man and have no demands to make, and *at the same time* that women will never be equal to men and that their demands are in vain. It is difficult for men to measure the enormous extent of social discrimination that seems insignificant from the outside and whose moral and intellectual repercussions are so deep in woman that they appear to spring from an original nature.† The man most sympathetic to women never knows her concrete situation fully. So there is no good reason to believe men when they try to defend privileges whose scope they cannot even fathom. We will not let ourselves be intimidated by the number and violence of attacks against women; nor be fooled by the self-serving praise showered on the "real woman"; nor be won over by men's enthusiasm for her destiny, a destiny they would not for the world want to share.

We must not, however, be any less mistrustful of feminists' arguments: very often their attempt to polemicize robs them of all value. If the "question of women" is so trivial, it is because masculine arrogance turned it into a "quarrel"; when people quarrel, they no longer reason well. What people have endlessly

---

* For example, man declares that he does not find his wife in any way diminished just because she does not have a profession: work in the home is just as noble, etc. Yet, at the first argument he remonstrates, "You wouldn't be able to earn a living without me."
† Describing this very process will be the object of Volume II of this study.

sought to prove is that woman is superior, inferior or equal to man: created after Adam, she is obviously a secondary being, some say; on the contrary, say others, Adam was only a rough draft, and God perfected the human being when he created Eve; her brain is smaller, but relatively bigger; Christ was made man: but perhaps out of humility. Every argument has its opposite and both are often misleading. To see clearly, one needs to get out of these ruts; these vague notions of superiority, inferiority and equality that have distorted all discussions must be discarded in order to start anew.

But how, then, will we ask the question? And in the first place, who are we to ask it? Men are judge and party: so are women. Can an angel be found? In fact, an angel would be ill-qualified to speak, would not understand all the givens of the problem; as for the hermaphrodite, it is a case of its own: it is not both a man and a woman, but neither man nor woman. I think certain women are still best suited to elucidate the situation of women. It is a sophism to claim that Epimenides should be enclosed within the concept of Cretan and all Cretans within the concept of liar: it is not a mysterious essence that dictates good or bad faith to men and women; it is their situation that disposes them to seek the truth to a greater or lesser extent. Many women today, fortunate to have had all the privileges of the human being restored to them, can afford the luxury of impartiality: we even feel the necessity of it. We are no longer like our militant predecessors;[24] we have more or less won the game; in the latest discussions on women's status, the UN has not ceased to imperiously demand equality of the sexes, and indeed many of us have never felt our femaleness to be a difficulty or an obstacle; many other problems seem more essential than those that concern us uniquely: this very detachment makes it possible to hope our attitude will be objective. Yet we know the feminine world more intimately than men do because our roots are in it; we grasp more immediately what the fact of being female means for a human being, and we care more about knowing it. I said that there are more essential problems; but this one still has a certain importance from our point of view: how will the fact of being women have affected our lives? What precise opportunities have been given us and which ones have been denied? What destiny awaits our younger sisters, and in which direction should we point them? It is striking that most feminine literature is driven today by an attempt at lucidity more than by a will to make demands; coming out of an era of muddled controversy, this book is one attempt among others to take stock of the current state.

But it is no doubt impossible to approach any human problem without partiality: even the way of asking the questions, of adopting perspectives, presupposes hierarchies of interests; all characteristics comprise values; every so-called objective description is set against an ethical background. Instead of trying to conceal those principles that are more or less explicitly implied, we would be better off stating them from the start; then it would not be necessary to specify on each page the meaning given to the words "superior," "inferior," "better," "worse," "progress," "regression," and so on. If we examine some of the books on women, we see that one of the most frequently held points of view is that of public good or general interest: in reality, this is taken to mean the interest of society as each one wishes to maintain or establish it. In our opinion, there is no public good other than one that assures the citizens' private good; we judge institutions from the point of view of the concrete opportunities they give to individuals. But neither do we confuse the idea of private interest with happiness: that is another frequently encountered point of view; are women in a harem not happier than a woman voter? Is a housewife not happier than a woman worker? We cannot really know what the word "happiness" means, and still less what authentic values it covers; there is no way to measure the happiness of others, and it is always easy to call a situation that one would like to impose on others happy: in particular, we declare happy those condemned to stagnation, under the pretext that happiness is immobility. This is a notion, then, we will not refer to. The perspective we have adopted is one of existentialist morality. Every subject posits itself as a transcendence concretely, through projects; it accomplishes its freedom only by perpetual surpassing toward other freedoms; there is no other justification for present existence than its expansion toward an indefinitely open future. Every time transcendence lapses into immanence, there is degradation of existence into "in-itself," of freedom into facticity; this fall is a moral fault if the subject consents to it; if this fall is inflicted on the subject, it takes the form of frustration and oppression; in both cases it is an absolute evil. Every individual concerned with justifying his existence experiences his existence as an indefinite need to transcend himself. But what singularly defines the situation of woman is that being, like all humans, an autonomous freedom, she discovers and chooses herself in a world where men force her to assume herself as Other: an attempt is made to freeze her as an object and doom her to immanence, since her transcendence will be forever transcended by another essential and sovereign consciousness. Woman's drama lies in this conflict between the fundamental claim of every subject, which always posits itself as essential, and the demands of a situation that constitutes her as inessential. How, in the feminine condition, can a human being accomplish herself? What paths are open to her? Which ones lead to dead ends? How can she find independence within dependence? What circumstances limit women's freedom and can she overcome them? These are the fundamental questions we would like to elucidate. This means that in focusing on the individual's possibilities, we will define these possibilities not in terms of happiness but in terms of freedom.

Clearly this problem would have no meaning if we

thought that a physiological, psychological or economic destiny weighed on woman. So we will begin by discussing woman from a biological, psychoanalytical and historical materialistic point of view. We will then attempt to positively demonstrate how "feminine reality" has been constituted, why woman has been defined as Other, and what the consequences have been from men's point of view. Then we will describe the world from the woman's point of view such as it is offered to her,[*] and we will see the difficulties women are up against just when, trying to escape the sphere they have been assigned until now, they seek to be part of the human *Mitsein*.

[*] This will be the subject of a second volume.

CHAPTER 14

THE INDEPENDENT WOMAN

French law no longer includes obedience among a wife's duties, and every woman citizen has become a voter;[1] these civic liberties remain abstract if there is no corresponding economic autonomy; the kept woman—wife or mistress—is not freed from the male just because she has a ballot paper in her hands; while today's customs impose fewer constraints on her than in the past, such negative licenses have not fundamentally changed her situation; she remains a vassal, imprisoned in her condition. It is through work that woman has been able, to a large extent, to close the gap separating her from the male; work alone can guarantee her concrete freedom. The system based on her dependence collapses as soon as she ceases to be a parasite; there is no longer need for a masculine mediator between her and the universe. The curse on the woman vassal is that she is not allowed to do anything; so she stubbornly pursues the impossible quest for being through narcissism, love or religion;[2] when she is productive and active, she regains her transcendence; she affirms herself concretely as subject in her projects; she senses her

31

responsibility relative to the goals she pursues and to the money and rights she appropriates. Many women are conscious of these advantages, even those with the lowest-level jobs. I heard a cleaning woman as she was washing a hotel lobby floor say, "I never asked anyone for anything. I made it on my own." She was as proud of being self-sufficient as a Rockefeller. However, one must not think that the simple juxtaposition of the right to vote and a job amounts to total liberation; work today is not freedom. Only in a socialist world would the woman who has one be sure of the other. Today, the majority of workers are exploited. Moreover, social structures have not been deeply modified by the changes in women's condition. This world has always belonged to men and still retains the form they have imprinted on it. It is important not to lose sight of these facts that make the question of women's work complex. An important and self-righteous woman recently carried out a study on women workers at a Renault factory: she asserts that they would rather stay at home than work in a factory. Without a doubt, they are economically independent only within an economically oppressed class; and besides, tasks carried out in a factory do not free them from household chores.* If they had been able to choose between forty hours of weekly work in a factory *or* at home, they would undoubtedly

* I said in Vol. I, Part Two, "History," chapter 5, how burdensome these are for the woman who works outside the home.[3]

have responded quite differently; and they might even accept both jobs eagerly if, as women workers, they would become part of a world that would be their world, that they would proudly and happily participate in building. In today's work, without even mentioning women who work on the land,[*] most working women do not escape the traditional feminine world; neither society nor their husbands give them the help needed to become, in concrete terms, the equals of men. Only those women with political convictions, active in trade unions, who are confident in the future, can give an ethical meaning to the thankless daily labor; but as women deprived of leisure time and inheriting a tradition of submissiveness, it is understandable that women are just beginning to develop their political and social awareness. It is understandable that since they do not receive the moral and social benefits they could legitimately expect in exchange for their work, they simply resign themselves to its constraints. It is also understandable that a shopgirl, an office worker or a secretary should not want to give up the advantages of having a male to lean on. I have already said that it is an almost irresistible temptation for a young woman to be part of a privileged caste when she can do so simply by surrendering her body; she is doomed to have love affairs because her wages are minimal for the very high standard of living society demands of her; if she settles for what she earns, she will be no

[*] Whose condition we examined, ibid.

more than a pariah: without decent living accommodation or clothes, all amusement and even love will be refused her. Virtuous people preach asceticism to her; in fact, her diet is often as austere as a Carmelite's; but not everyone can have God as a lover: she needs to please men to succeed in her life as a woman. So she will accept help: her employer cynically counts on this when he pays her a pittance. Sometimes this help will enable her to improve her situation and achieve real independence; but sometimes she will give up her job to become a kept woman. She often does both: she frees herself from her lover through work, and she escapes work thanks to her lover; but then she experiences the double servitude of a job and masculine protection. For the married woman, her salary usually only means extra income; for the "woman who is helped" it is the man's protection that seems inessential; but neither woman buys total independence through her own efforts.

However, there are quite a lot of privileged women today who have gained economic and social autonomy in their professions. They are the ones who are at issue when the question of women's possibilities and their future is raised. While they are still only a minority, it is particularly interesting to study their situation closely; they are the subject of continuing debate between feminists and antifeminists. The latter maintain that today's emancipated women do not accomplish anything important, and that besides they have trouble finding their inner balance. The former exaggerate the emancipated women's achievements and are blind to their frustrations. In fact, there is no reason to assume that they are on the wrong track; and yet it is obvious that they are not comfortably settled in their new condition: they have come only halfway as yet. Even the woman who has emancipated herself economically from man is still not in a moral, social or psychological situation identical to his. Her commitment to and focus on her profession depend on the context of her life as a whole. And, when she starts her adult life, she does not have the same past as a boy; society does not see her with the same eyes; she has a different perspective on the universe. Being a woman poses unique problems to an autonomous human being today.

The advantage man enjoys and which manifests itself from childhood onwards is that his vocation as a human being in no way contradicts his destiny as a male. The fact that the phallus is assimilated with transcendence means that man's social and spiritual successes endow him with virile prestige. He is not divided. However, for a woman to accomplish her femininity she is required to be object and prey; that is, she must renounce her claims as a sovereign subject. This is the conflict that singularly characterizes the situation of the emancipated woman. She refuses to confine herself to her role as female because she does not want to mutilate herself; but it would also be a mutilation to repudiate her sex. Man is a sexed human being; woman is a complete individual, and equal to the male, only if she too is a sexed human being. Renouncing her femininity means renouncing part of her humanity. Misogynists have often reproached intellectual women for "letting themselves go"; but they also preach to them: if you want to be our equals, stop wearing makeup and polishing your nails. This advice is absurd. Precisely because the idea of femininity is artificially defined by customs and fashion, it is imposed on every woman from the outside; it may evolve so that its fashion standards come closer to those of men: on the beach, women now wear trousers. That does not change the core of the problem: the individual is not free to shape the idea of femininity at will. By not conforming, a woman devalues herself sexually and consequently socially because society has incorporated sexual values. Rejecting feminine attributes does not mean acquiring virile ones; even a transvestite cannot turn herself into a man: she is a transvestite. We have seen[4] that homosexuality also constitutes a specification: neutrality is impossible. There is no negative attitude that does not imply a positive counterpart. The adolescent girl often thinks she can simply scorn convention; but by doing so, she is making a statement; she is creating a new situation involving consequences she will have to assume.[5] Whenever one ignores an established convention, one becomes a rebel. A flamboyantly dressed woman is lying when she ingenuously claims she is simply dressing to suit herself, and that is all: she knows perfectly well that suiting herself is an absurdity. Inversely, if

36

she does not want to look eccentric, she follows the rules. Choosing defiance is a risky tactic unless it is a positively effective action; more time and energy are spent than saved. A woman who has no desire to shock, no intention to devalue herself socially, has to live her woman's condition as a woman: very often her professional success even requires it. But while conformity is quite natural for a man—custom being based on his needs as an autonomous and active individual—the woman who is herself also subject and activity has to fit into a world that has doomed her to passivity. This servitude is even greater since women confined to the feminine sphere have magnified its importance: they have made dressing and housekeeping difficult arts. The man barely has to care about his clothes; they are comfortable, adapted to his active life, and need not be original; they are hardly part of his personality; what's more, no one expects him to take care of them himself: some woman, volunteer or paid, delivers him from this chore. The woman, on the other hand, knows that when people look at her, they do not distinguish her from her appearance: she is judged, respected or desired in relation to how she looks. Her clothes were originally meant to doom her to impotence, and they still remain fragile: stockings run; heels wear down; light-colored blouses and dresses get dirty; pleats unpleat; but she must still repair most of these accidents herself; her peers will never volunteer to help her out, and she will have second thoughts about straining her budget for work she *can* do herself: perms, hairdos, makeup and new dresses are already expensive enough. Secretary or student, when she goes home at night, there is always a stocking to mend, a blouse to wash, a skirt to iron. The woman who earns a good living will spare herself these chores; but she will be held to a higher standard of elegance, she will waste time on shopping and dress fittings, and such. Tradition also demands that the woman, even unmarried, pay attention to her home; a government official sent to a new city thinks nothing of living in a hotel; his woman colleague will try to "set up house"; she has to keep it spotless because her negligence will not be excused whereas a man's will be overlooked. However, public opinion is not the only concern that makes her devote so much time and care to her looks and home. She wants to feel like a real woman for her own personal satisfaction. She only succeeds in accepting herself from the perspective of both the present and the past by combining the life she has made for herself with the destiny prepared for her by her mother, her childhood games and her adolescent fantasies. She has cultivated narcissistic dreams; she continues to pit the cult of her image against the phallic pride of the male; she wants to show off, to charm. Her mother and other older women have fostered her nesting instinct: a home of her own was the earliest form of her dream of independence; she would not think of discarding it, even when she finds freedom in other ways. And not yet feeling secure in the male universe, she still needs a retreat, a symbol of that interior refuge she has been used to finding in herself. Following docilely in the feminine tradition, she will wax her floors or do her own cooking instead of going to a restaurant like her male colleague. She wants to live both like a man and like a woman; her workload and her fatigue are multiplied as a result.

If she intends to remain fully woman, it also means she intends to approach the opposite sex with the maximum of odds on her side. It is in the area of sex that the most difficult problems will arise. To be a complete individual, equal to man, woman has to have access to the male world as man does to the female one, access to the *other*; but the demands of the *other* are not symmetrical in the two cases. Once acquired, the seemingly immanent virtues of fame and fortune can enhance the woman's sexual attraction; but being an autonomous activity contradicts her femininity: she knows this. The independent woman—and especially the intellectual who thinks through her situation—will suffer from an inferiority complex as a female; she does not have as much free time for beauty care as a flirt, whose only preoccupation is to seduce; while she might follow all the experts' advice, she will never be more than an amateur in the elegance department; feminine charm demands that transcendence deteriorating into immanence no longer be anything more than a subtle carnal throb, she must be a spontaneously offered prey: the intellectual woman knows she is offering herself, she knows she is a consciousness, a subject; one cannot willfully kill one's gaze and change one's eyes into empty pools; a body that reaches out to the world cannot be thwarted and metamorphosed into a statue animated by hidden vibrations. The more the intellectual woman fears failure, the more zealously she will try; but this conscious zeal remains an activity and falls short of its goal. She makes mistakes like those blamed on menopause: she tries to deny her intelligence as an aging woman tries to deny her age; she dresses like a girl, she overdoes the flowers, the frills and the loud materials; she carries childish and wide-eyed mimicry too far. She romps, skips, prattles, acts overly casual, scatterbrained and impulsive. But she looks like those actors who, failing to feel the emotion that would relax certain muscles, purposely contract antagonistic ones instead, lowering their eyelids or the corners of their mouths instead of letting them drop; thus the intelligent woman, wishing to appear uninhibited, stiffens instead. She senses this, and it irritates her; suddenly an unintended piercing spark of intelligence passes over her totally naive face; her lips full of promise become pursed. If she has trouble pleasing men, it is because she is not like her little slave sisters, a pure will to please; her desire to seduce may be strong, but it has not penetrated into the marrow of her bones; as soon as she feels awkward, she gets fed up with her servility; she tries to take her revenge by playing the game with masculine weapons: she talks instead of listening, she flaunts clever ideas, unusual feelings; she contradicts her interlocutor instead of going along with him, she tries to outdo him. Mme de Staël cleverly mixed both methods with stunning triumphs: she was almost always irresistible. But defiance, so frequent, for example, among American women, irritates men more than it wins them over; it is men, however, who provoke it by their own defiance; if men were content to love a peer instead of a slave—as indeed some men do who are without either arrogance or an inferiority complex—then women would be far less obsessed with their femininity; they would become more natural and simple and would easily rediscover themselves as women, which, after all, they are.

The fact is that men are beginning to come to terms with the new condition of women; no longer feeling condemned a priori, women feel more at ease; today the working woman does not neglect her femininity, nor does she lose her sexual attraction. This success—already a step toward equality—remains, nonetheless, incomplete; it is still much harder for a woman than for a man to have the type of relationship she would like with the other sex. Many obstacles stand in the way of her sex and love life. And the vassal woman is no better off: sexually and emotionally, most wives and mistresses are radically frustrated. These difficulties are more obvious for the independent woman because she has chosen not resignation but combat. All living problems find a silent solution in death; so a woman who works at living is more torn than one who buries her will and desires; but she will not accept being offered this as an example. She will consider herself at a disadvantage only when she compares herself with man.

A woman who works hard, who has responsibilities and who knows how harsh the struggle is against the world's obstacles needs—like the male—not only to satisfy her physical desires but also to experience the relaxation and diversion provided by enjoyable sexual adventures. Now there are still some environments where it is not concretely recognized that she should have this freedom; if she avails herself of it, she risks compromising her reputation and career; at the least, a burdensome hypocrisy is demanded of her. The more she has succeeded in making her mark socially, the more willingly will people close their eyes; but she is severely scrutinized, especially in the provinces. Even in the most favorable circumstances—when fear of public opinion is not an issue—her situation is not the same in this area as the man's. Differences stem from both tradition and the problems posed by the particular nature of feminine sexuality.

The man can easily engage in casual sex that at least calms his physical needs and is good for his morale. There have been women—a small number— who have demanded the opening of bordellos for women; in a novel entitled *Number 17*, a woman proposed creating houses where women could go and find "sexual relief" with a sort of "taxi-boy."* It seems that such an establishment once existed in San Francisco; it was frequented only by the girls from the bordellos, amused by the idea of paying instead of being paid: their pimps had them closed. Besides the fact that this solution is utopian and undesirable, it would also probably have little success: we have seen[6] that woman does not attain "relief" as mechanically as man; most women would hardly consider this solution favorable to sexual abandon. In any case, the fact is that this recourse is not open to them today. The solution of women picking up a partner for a night or an hour—assuming that the woman, endowed with a strong temperament and having overcome all her inhibitions, can consider it without disgust is far more dangerous for her than for the male. The risk of venereal disease is more serious for her in that it is up to him to take precautions to avoid contamination; and, however prudent she may be, she is never completely covered against the threat of becoming pregnant.[7] But the difference in physical strength is also very significant, especially in relations between strangers—relations that take place on a physical level. A man has little to fear from the woman he takes home; a little vigilance is enough. It is not the same for the woman who lets a man into her house. I

* The author—whose name I have forgotten, but it is unimportant—explains at length how they could be trained to satisfy any client, what kind of life should be imposed on them, and so forth.

have been told of two young women, newly arrived in Paris and avid to "see life," who, after doing the town, invited two seductive Montmartre pimps to a late supper: in the morning they found themselves robbed, brutalized and threatened with blackmail. A worse case is that of a divorced woman of about forty who worked hard all day to feed her three grown children and elderly parents. Still beautiful and attractive, she had absolutely no leisure time to have a social life, to flirt or to make any of the usual efforts necessary for seduction, which in any case would have bored her. Yet she had strong physical desires; and she felt that, like a man, she had the right to satisfy them. Some evenings she went out to roam the streets and managed to pick up a man. But one night, after an hour or two spent in a thicket in the Bois de Boulogne, her lover refused to let her leave: he wanted her name, her address, to see her again, to live with her; when she refused, he beat her violently and only left her when she was wounded and terrorized. As for taking on a lover by supporting him or helping him out, as men often take on a mistress, it is possible only for wealthy women. There are some for whom this deal works: by paying the male, they make an instrument of him, permitting them to use him with disdainful abandon. But women must usually be older to dissociate eroticism from sentiment so crudely, because in feminine adolescence this connection is, as we have seen,[8] so deep. There are also many men who never accept this division between flesh and consciousness.

For even more reasons, the majority of women will refuse to consider it. Besides, there is an element of deception they are more aware of than men: the paying client is an instrument as well, used by the partner as a livelihood. Virile arrogance hides the ambiguities of the erotic drama from the male: he spontaneously lies to himself; the woman is more easily humiliated, more susceptible, and also more lucid; she will succeed in blinding herself only at the price of a more cunning bad faith. Even supposing she has the means, she will not find it generally satisfying to buy a man.

For most women—and also for some men—it is a question not only of satisfying their desires but of maintaining their dignity as human beings while satisfying them. When the male gets sexual satisfaction from the woman, or when he satisfies her, he posits himself as the unique subject: imperious victor, generous donor, or both. She wants to affirm reciprocally that she submits her partner to her pleasure and covers him with her gifts. Thus when she convinces the man of her worth, either by the benefits she promises him or by relying on his courtesy or by skillfully arousing his desire in its pure generality, she easily persuades herself that she is satisfying him. Thanks to this beneficial conviction, she can solicit him without feeling humiliated since she claims she is acting out of generosity. Thus in *Green Wheat*,[9] the "woman in white" who lusts for Phil's caresses archly tells him: "I only like beggars and the hungry." In fact, she is cleverly angling for him to act imploringly. So, says

Colette, "She rushed toward the narrow and dark kingdom where her pride could believe that a moan is a confession of distress and where the aggressive beggars of her sort drink the illusion of generosity." Mme de Warens[10] exemplifies these women who choose their lovers young, unhappy or of a lower social class to make their appetite look like generosity. But there are also fearless women who take on the challenge of the most robust males and who are delighted to have satisfied them even though they may have succumbed only out of politeness or fear.

On the other hand, while the woman who traps the man likes to imagine herself giving, the woman who gives herself wants it understood that she takes. "As for me, I am a woman who takes," a young woman journalist told me one day. The truth in these cases is that, except for rape, no one really takes the other; but the woman is lying doubly to herself. For the fact is that man does often seduce by his passion and aggressiveness, thereby actively gaining his partner's consent. Except in special cases—like Mme de Staël, to whom I have already referred—it is otherwise for the woman: she can do little else than offer herself; for most males are fiercely jealous of their role; they want to awaken a personal sexual response in the woman, not to be selected to satisfy her need in its generality: chosen, they feel exploited.* "A woman who is not

* This feeling corresponds to the one we have pointed out in the girl. Only she resigns herself to her destiny in the end.

afraid of men frightens them," a young man told me. And I have often heard adults declare: "I am horrified by a woman who takes the initiative." If the woman proposes herself too boldly, the man flees: he insists on conquering. The woman can thus take only when she is prey: she must become a passive thing, a promise of submission. If she succeeds, she will think she has willingly performed this magic conjuration; she will see herself become subject again. But she runs the risk of being turned into a fixed and useless object by the male's disdain. This is why she is so deeply humiliated if he rejects her advances. The man also sometimes gets angry when he feels he has been taken in; nonetheless, he has only failed in an enterprise, nothing more. The woman, on the other hand, has consented to make herself flesh through her sexual arousal, anticipation and promise; she could only win by losing: she remains lost. One must be particularly blind or exceptionally lucid to choose such a defeat. And even when seduction succeeds, victory remains ambiguous; thus, according to public opinion, it is the man who conquers, who *has* the woman. It does not accept that she can, like the man, assume her desires: she is their prey. It is understood that the male has integrated the forces of the species into his individuality, whereas the woman is the slave of the species.*

* We have seen in Vol. 1, Chapter I, that there is a certain truth in this opinion. But it is precisely not at the moment of desire that this asymmetry appears: it is in procreation. In desire man and woman assume their natural function identically.

She is represented alternately as pure passivity: she is a "slut; open for business"; ready and willing, she is a utensil; she limply gives in to the spell of arousal, she is fascinated by the male who picks her like a fruit. Or else she is seen as an alienated activity: there is a devil raging in her womb, a serpent lurks in her vagina, craving to devour male sperm. In any case, it is out of the question to think of her as simply free. In France especially, the free woman and the easy woman are stubbornly confused, as the idea of easy implies an absence of resistance and control, a lack, the very negation of freedom. Women authors try to combat this prejudice: for example, in *Portrait of Grisela*,[11] Clara Malraux emphasizes that her heroine does not let herself be drawn in, but accomplishes an act for which she accepts full responsibility. In America, a freedom is recognized in woman's sexual activity, which is very favorable to her. But in France, men's disdain for women who "sleep around," the very men who profit from their favors, paralyzes many women. They fear the remonstrances they would incite, the remarks they would provoke.

Even if the woman scorns anonymous rumors, she has concrete difficulties in her relations with her partner, for public opinion is embodied in him. Very often, he considers the bed the terrain for asserting his aggressive superiority. He wants to take and not receive, not exchange but ravish. He seeks to possess the woman beyond that which she gives him; he demands that her consent be a defeat, and that the

48

words she murmurs be avowals that he extracts from her; if she admits her pleasure, she is acknowledging her submission. When Claudine defies Renaud by her promptness in submitting to him, he anticipates her: he rushes to rape her when she was going to offer herself; he forces her to keep her eyes open to contemplate his triumph in their torment. Thus, in *Man's Fate*,[12] the overbearing Ferral insists on switching on the lamp Valérie wants to put out. Proud and demanding, the woman faces the male as an adversary; she is far less well armed in this battle than he; first of all, he has physical force and it is easier for him to impose his desires; we have also noted that tension and activity correspond to his eroticism, whereas the woman who refuses passivity breaks the spell that brings her sexual satisfaction; if she mimics domination in her attitudes and movements, she fails to reach a climax: most women who surrender to their pride become frigid. Rare are those lovers who allow their mistresses to satisfy their dominating or sadistic tendencies; and even rarer still are those women who derive full erotic satisfaction from this male docility.

There is a road that seems much less thorny for the woman, that of masochism. When one works, struggles and takes responsibilities and risks during the day, it is relaxing to abandon oneself at night to vigorous caprices. In love or naive, the woman in fact is often happy to annihilate herself for the benefit of a tyrannical will. But she still has to feel truly dominated. It is not easy for a woman who lives daily among men

49

to believe in the unconditional supremacy of males. I have been told about the case of a not really masochistic but very "feminine" woman, that is, one who deeply appreciated the pleasure of abdication in masculine arms; from the age of seventeen, she had had several husbands and numerous lovers, all of whom gave her great satisfaction; having successfully carried out a difficult project where she managed men, she complained of having become frigid: her once-blissful submission became impossible for her because she had become used to dominating males and because their prestige had vanished. When the woman begins to doubt men's superiority, their claims can only diminish her esteem for them. In bed, at moments where the man feels he is most fiercely male, the very fact of his miming virility makes him look infantile to knowing eyes: he is merely warding off the old castration complex, the shadow of his father, or some other fantasy. It is not always out of pride that the mistress refuses to give in to her lover's caprices: she wants to interact with an adult who is living a real moment of his life, not a little boy fooling himself. The masochistic woman is particularly disappointed: a maternal, exasperated or indulgent complaisance is not the abdication she dreams of. Either she herself will also have to make do with meaningless games, pretending to be dominated and subjugated, or she will run after men considered "superior" in the hope of coming across a master, or else she will become frigid.

We have seen[13] that it is possible to escape the

50

temptations of sadism and masochism when both partners recognize each other as equals; as soon as there is a little modesty and some generosity between men and women, ideas of victory and defeat are abolished: the act of love becomes a free exchange. But, paradoxically, it is harder for woman than for man to recognize an individual of the opposite sex as her equal. Precisely because the male caste enjoys superiority, man can hold many individual women in affectionate esteem: a woman is easy to love; she has, first of all, the privilege of introducing her lover to a world different from his own and one that he is pleased to explore at her side; she fascinates, she amuses, at least for a little while; and then, because her situation is limited and subordinate, all her qualities seem like conquests while her errors are excusable. Stendhal[14] admires Mme de Rênal and Mme de Chasteller in spite of their detestable prejudices; the man does not hold a woman responsible for not being very intelligent, clear-sighted or courageous: she is a victim, he thinks—often rightly—of her situation; he dreams of what she could have been, of what she will perhaps be: she can be given credit, one can grant her a great deal because she *is* nothing definite in particular; this lack is what will cause the lover to grow tired of her quickly: but it is the source of her mystery, the charm that seduces him and inclines him to feel superficial tenderness for her. It is far less easy to show friendship for a man: for he is what he made himself be, without help; he must be loved in his presence and his reality, not in his promises and uncertain possibilities; he is responsible for his behavior, his ideas; he has no excuse. There is fraternity with him only if his acts, goals and opinions are approved; Julien can love a legitimist; a Lamiel could not cherish a man whose ideas she detests. Even ready to compromise, the woman has trouble adopting a tolerant attitude. For the man does not offer her a green paradise of childhood, she meets him in this world that is common to both of them: he brings only himself. Closed in on himself, defined, decided, he does not inspire dreams; when he speaks, one must listen; he takes himself seriously: if he does not prove interesting, he becomes bothersome, his presence weighs heavily. Only very young men allow themselves to appear adorned by the marvelous; one can seek mystery and promise in them, find excuses for them, take them lightly: this is one of the reasons mature women find them so seductive. But they themselves prefer young women in most cases. The thirty-year-old woman has no choice but to turn to adult males. And she will undoubtedly meet some who deserve both her esteem and her friendship; but she will be lucky if they do not then display arrogance. The problem she has when looking for an affair or an adventure involving her heart as well as her body is meeting a man she can consider her equal, without his seeing himself as superior.

One might say that in general women do not make such a fuss; they seize the occasion without much questioning, and then they make do with their pride and sensuality. That is true. But it is also true that they bury in the secret of their hearts many disappointments, humiliations, regrets and grievances whose equivalents are unknown—on the whole—to men. The man will almost surely get the benefit of pleasure from a more or less unsuccessful affair; the woman might well not profit from it at all; even if indifferent, she politely lends herself to lovemaking when the decisive moment arrives. The lover might prove to be impotent, and she will suffer from having compromised herself in a ludicrous escapade; if she does not reach arousal, then she feels "had," deceived; if she is satisfied, she will want to hold on to her lover for a longer time. She is rarely completely sincere when she claims to envisage nothing more than a short-term adventure just for pleasure, because pleasure, far from freeing her, binds her; separation, even a so-called friendly one, wounds her. It is far more rare to hear a woman talk good-naturedly about a former lover than a man about his mistresses.

The nature of her eroticism and the difficulties of a free sexual life push the woman toward monogamy. Nonetheless, a liaison or marriage is far less easily reconciled with a career for her than for the man. The lover or husband may ask her to give up her career: she hesitates, like Colette's Vagabond[15] who ardently wishes to have a man's warmth at her side but who dreads the conjugal shackles; if she gives in, she is once again a vassal; if she refuses, she condemns herself to a withering solitude. Today, the man generally accepts the idea that his partner should continue working; novels by Colette Yver[16] that show young women cornered into sacrificing their professions to maintain peace at home are somewhat outdated; living together is an enrichment for two free beings, who find a guarantee of their own independence in the partner's occupations; the self-sufficient wife frees her husband from the conjugal slavery that was the price of her own. If the man is scrupulously well-intentioned, lovers and spouses can attain perfect equality in undemanding generosity.* Sometimes the man himself plays the role of devoted servant; thus did Lewes create for George Eliot[17] the favorable atmosphere the wife usually creates around the lord-husband. But most of the time, it is still the woman who pays the price for harmony at home. It seems natural to the man that she run the house and over-see the care and raising of the children alone. The woman herself believes that her personal life does not dispense her from the duties she assumed in marry-ing; she does not want her husband to be deprived of the advantages he would have had in marrying a "real woman": she wants to be elegant, a good housekeeper and devoted mother as wives traditionally are. It is a task that easily becomes overwhelming. She assumes it out of both consideration for her partner and fidelity to herself: for she insists, as we have seen,[18] on fulfill-

---

* Clara and Robert Schumann's life seems to have had this kind of success for a certain time.

ing every aspect of her destiny as woman. She will be a double for her husband at the same time as being herself; she will take charge of his worries, she will participate in his successes just as much as taking care of her own lot, and sometimes even more so. Taught to respect male superiority, she may still believe that man takes first place; and sometimes she fears that claiming it would ruin her family; split between the desire to affirm herself and self-effacement, she is divided and torn.

There is nonetheless one advantage woman can gain from her very inferiority: since from the start she has fewer chances than man, she does not feel a priori guilty toward him; it is not up to her to compensate for social injustice, and she is not called upon to do so. A man of goodwill feels it his duty to "help" women because he is more favored than they are; he will let himself be caught up in scruples or pity, and he risks being the prey of "clinging" or "devouring" women because they are at a disadvantage. The woman who achieves a virile independence has the great privilege of dealing sexually with autonomous and active individuals who—generally—will not play a parasite's role in her life, who will not bind her by their weaknesses and the demands of their needs. But women who know how to create a free relation with their partners are in truth rare; they themselves forge the chains with which men do not wish to burden them: they adopt toward their partner the attitude of the woman in love. For twenty years of waiting, dreaming and hoping, the young girl has embraced the myth of the liberating hero and savior: independence won through work is not enough to abolish her desire for a glorious abdication. She would have had to be brought up exactly like a boy[*] to be able to comfortably overcome adolescent narcissism: but in her adult life she perpetuates this cult of self toward which her whole youth has predisposed her; she uses the merits of her professional success to enrich her image; she needs a gaze from above to reveal and consecrate her worth. Even if she is severe on men whom she judges daily, she reveres Man nonetheless and if she encounters him, she is ready to fall on her knees. To be justified by a god is easier than to be justified by her own effort; the world encourages her to believe in the possibility of a *given* salvation: she chooses to believe in it. At times she entirely renounces her autonomy, she is no more than a woman in love; more often she tries conciliation; but adoring love, the love of abdication, is devastating: it takes up all thoughts, all instants, it is obsessive, tyrannical. If she encounters a professional disappointment, the woman passionately seeks refuge in love: her failures find expression in scenes and demands at the lover's expense. But her heartbreaks in no way have the effect of increasing her professional zeal: generally she becomes irritated, on the contrary, by the kind of life that keeps her from the royal road

* That is, not only with the same methods, but in the same climate, which today is impossible in spite of all the efforts of educators.

of the great love. A woman who worked ten years ago for a political magazine run by women told me that in the office people talked rarely about politics but incessantly about love: one would complain that she was loved only for her body, ignoring her fine intelligence; another would whine that she was only appreciated for her mind and no one ever appreciated her physical charms. Here again, for the woman to be in love like a man—that is to say, without putting her very *being* into question, freely—she would have to think herself his equal, and be his equal concretely: she would have to commit herself with the same decisiveness to her enterprises, which, as we will see, is still not common.

There is one female function that is still almost impossible to undertake in complete freedom, and that is motherhood; in England and in America, the woman can at least refuse it at will, thanks to the practice of birth control;[19] we have seen that in France she is often compelled to have painful and costly abortions;[20] she often finds herself burdened with a child she did not want, ruining her professional life. If this burden is a heavy one, it is because, inversely, social norms do not allow the woman to procreate as she pleases: the unwed mother causes scandal and for the child an illegitimate birth is a stain; it is rare for a woman to become a mother without accepting the chains of marriage or lowering herself. If the idea of artificial insemination interests women so much, it is not because they wish to avoid male lovemaking: it is because they hope that voluntary motherhood will

57

finally be accepted by society. It must be added that given the lack of well-organized day nurseries and kindergartens, even one child is enough to entirely paralyze a woman's activity; she can continue to work only by abandoning the child to her parents, friends or servants. She has to choose between sterility, often experienced as a painful frustration, and burdens hardly compatible with a career.

Thus the independent woman today is divided between her professional interests and the concerns of her sexual vocation; she has trouble finding her balance; if she does, it is at the price of concessions, sacrifices and juggling that keep her in constant tension. More than in physiological facts, it is here that one must seek the reason for the nervousness and frailty often observed in her. It is difficult to decide how much woman's physical makeup in itself represents a handicap. The obstacle created by menstruation, for example, has often been examined. Women known for their work or activities seem to attach little importance to it: is this because they owe their success to the fact that their monthly problems are so mild? One may ask if it is not on the contrary the choice of an active and ambitious life that confers this privilege on them: the attention women pay to their ailments exacerbates them; athletic women and women of action suffer less than the others because they pass over their sufferings. It is clear that menstrual pain does have organic causes, and I have seen the most energetic women spend twenty-four hours in bed every month in the throes of pitiless tortures; but their enterprises were never hindered by them. I am convinced that most ailments and illnesses that weigh women down have psychic causes: this is in fact what gynecologists have told me. Women are constantly overwhelmed by the psychological tension I have spoken about, because of all the tasks they take on and the contradictions they struggle against; this does not mean that their ills are imaginary: they are as real and devouring as the situation they convey. But a situation does not depend on the body, it is rather the body that depends on it. So woman's health will not detract from her work when the working woman has the place she deserves in society; on the contrary work will strongly reinforce her physical balance by keeping her from being endlessly preoccupied with it.

When we judge the professional accomplishments of women and try to speculate on their future on that basis, we must not lose sight of all these facts. The woman embarks on a career in the context of a highly problematic situation, subjugated still by the burdens traditionally implied by her femininity. Objective circumstances are no more favorable to her either. It is always hard to be a newcomer trying to make one's way in a hostile society, or at least a mistrustful one. Richard Wright showed in *Black Boy*[21] how blocked from the start the ambitions of a young American black man are and what struggle he has to endure merely to raise himself to the level where whites begin to have problems; the blacks who came to France from

Africa also have—within themselves as well as from outside—difficulties similar to those encountered by women.

The woman first finds herself in a state of inferiority during her period of apprenticeship: I have already pointed this out in relation to the period of girlhood, but it must be dealt with in more detail. During her studies and in the early decisive years of her career, it is rare for the woman to be able to make full use of her possibilities: many will later be handicapped by a bad start. In fact, the conflicts I have discussed will reach their greatest intensity between the ages of eighteen and thirty: and this is when their professional future is determined. Whether the woman lives with her family or is married, her friends and family will rarely respect her efforts as they respect a man's; they will impose duties and chores on her, and curtail her freedom; she herself is still profoundly marked by her upbringing, respectful of the values the older women around her represent, haunted by childhood and adolescent dreams; she has difficulty reconciling the inheritance of her past with the interest of her future. Sometimes she rejects her femininity, she hesitates between chastity, homosexuality or a provocative virago attitude, she dresses badly or like a man: she wastes a lot of time and energy in defiance, scenes and anger. More often she wants, on the contrary, to assert her femininity: she dresses up, goes out and flirts, she is in love, wavering between masochism and aggressiveness. In all cases, she questions herself, is agitated and scattered. By the very fact that she is in thrall to outside preoccupations, she does not commit herself entirely to her enterprise; thus she profits from it less, and is more tempted to give it up. What is extremely demoralizing for the woman trying to be self-sufficient is the existence of other women of her class, having from the start the same situation and chances, and who live as parasites; the man might resent privileged people: but he feels solidarity with his class; on the whole, those who begin on an equal footing with equal chances arrive at approximately the same standard of living, while women in similar situations have greatly differing fortunes because of man's mediation; the woman friend who is married or comfortably kept is a temptation for the woman who has to ensure her success alone; she feels she is arbitrarily condemning herself to the most difficult paths: at each obstacle she wonders if it would not be better to choose a different way. "When I think I have to get everything from my brain!" a young, poor student told me indignantly. The man obeys an imperious necessity: the woman must constantly renew her decision; she goes forward, not with her eye fixed on a goal directly in front of her, but letting her attention wander all around her; thus her progress is timid and uncertain. And moreover—as I have already said—it seems to her that the farther she advances, the more she renounces her other chances; in becoming a bluestocking, a cerebral woman, she will either displease men in general or humiliate her husband or lover by being too dazzling a success. Not only will she apply herself all the more to appearing elegant and frivolous, but she will also hold herself back. The hope of one day being free from looking after herself and the fear of having to give up this hope by coping with this anxiety come together to prevent her from devoting herself single-mindedly to her studies and career.

Inasmuch as the woman wants to be woman, her independent status produces an inferiority complex; inversely, her femininity leads her to doubt her professional opportunities. This is a most important point. A study showed that fourteen-year-old girls believed: "Boys are better; they find it easier to work." The girl is convinced that she has limited capacities. Because parents and teachers accept that the girl's level is lower than the boy's, students readily accept it too; and in truth, in spite of the fact that the curricula are identical, girls' intellectual growth in secondary schools is given less importance. With few exceptions, the students in a female philosophy class overall have a markedly lower achievement level than a class of boys: many female students do not intend to continue their studies, they work superficially and others suffer from a lack of competitiveness. As long as the exams are fairly easy, their inadequacy will not be noticed too much; but when serious competitive exams are in question, the female student will become aware of her weaknesses; she will attribute them to the unjust curse of femaleness and not to the mediocrity of her education; resigning herself to inequality, she exacerbates it; she persuades herself that her chances of success are related to her patience and assiduity; she decides to use her strength sparingly: this is a bad calculation. Above all, in studies and professions requiring a degree of inventiveness, originality and some small discoveries, a utilitarian attitude is disastrous; conversations, reading outside the syllabus, or a walk that allows the mind to wander freely can be far more profitable even for the translation of a Greek text than the dreary compilation of complex syntaxes. Crushed by respect for those in authority and the weight of erudition, her vision blocked by blinkers, the overly conscientious female student kills her critical sense and even her intelligence. Her methodical determination gives rise to tension and ennui: in classes where female secondary school students prepare for the Sèvres[22] examination, there is a stifling atmosphere that discourages even slightly spirited individuality. Having created her own jail, the female examination candidate wants nothing more than to escape from it; as soon as she closes her books, she thinks about any other subject. She does not experience those rich moments where study and amusement merge, where adventures of the mind acquire living warmth. Overwhelmed by the thanklessness of her chores, she feels less and less able to carry them out. I remember a female student doing the *agrégation* who said, at the time when there was a coed competitive exam in philosophy: "Boys can succeed in one or two years; we need at least four."

Another—who was recommended a book on Kant, a writer on the curriculum—commented: "This book is too difficult: It's for Normalians!" She seemed to think that women could take easier exams; beaten before even trying, she was in effect giving all chances of success to the men.

Because of this defeatist attitude, the woman easily settles for a mediocre success; she does not dare to aim higher. Starting out in her job with a superficial education, she very quickly curtails her ambitions. She often considers the very fact of earning her own living a great enough feat; like so many others, she could have entrusted her future to a man; to continue to want her independence she needs to take pride in her effort but it exhausts her. It seems to her she has done enough just in choosing to do something. "That's not so bad for a woman," she thinks. A woman in an unusual profession said: "If I were a man, I would feel obliged to be in the top rank; but I am the only woman in France holding such a position: that's enough for me." There is prudence in her modesty. In trying to go further, the woman is afraid of failing miserably. She is bothered, and rightly so, by the idea that no one has confidence in her. In general, the superior caste is hostile to the parvenus of the inferior caste: whites will not go to see a black doctor, nor men a woman doctor; but individuals from the lower caste, imbued with the feeling of their generic inferiority and often full of resentment of someone who has prevailed over destiny, will also prefer to turn to the masters; in particular, most women, steeped in the adoration of the male, avidly seek him in the doctor, lawyer, office manager. Neither men nor women like working under a woman's orders. Even if her superiors appreciate her, they will always be somewhat condescending; to be a woman is, if not a defect, at least a peculiarity. The woman must ceaselessly earn a confidence not initially granted to her: at the outset she is suspect; she has to prove herself. If she is any good, she will, people say. But worth is not a given essence: it is the result of a favorable development. Feeling a negative judgment weighing on one rarely helps one to overcome it. The initial inferiority complex most usually leads to the defensive reaction of an exaggerated affectation of authority. Most women doctors, for example, have too much or too little. If they are natural, they are not intimidating because their life as a whole disposes them more to seduce than to command; the patient who likes to be dominated will be disappointed by advice simply given; conscious of this, the woman doctor uses a low voice, a decisive tone, but then she does not have the cheerful simplicity that is so seductive in the confident doctor. The man is used to being imposing; his clients believe in his competence; he can let himself go: he is sure to impress. The woman does not inspire the same feeling of security; she stiffens, exaggerates, overdoes it. In business, in the office, she is scrupulous, a stickler and easily aggressive. Just as she is in her studies, she lacks confidence, inspiration and daring. In an effort to succeed she becomes tense.

Her behavior is a series of provocations and abstract self-affirmations. The greatest failure a lack of self-assurance brings about is that the subject cannot forget himself. He does not generously aim for a goal: he tries to prove he is worth what is demanded of him. Throwing oneself boldly toward goals risks setbacks: but one also attains unexpected results; prudence necessarily leads to mediocrity It is rare to see in the woman a taste for adventure, gratuitous experience or disinterested curiosity; she seeks "to build a career" the way others construct a happy life; she remains dominated, invested by the male universe, she lacks the audacity to break through the ceiling, she does not passionately lose herself in her projects; she still considers her life an immanent enterprise: she aims not for an object, but through an object for her subjective success. This is a very striking attitude in, among others, American women; it pleases them to have a job and to prove to themselves they are able to carry it out properly: but they do not become passionate about the *content* of their tasks. Likewise, the woman has a tendency to attach too much importance to minor failures and modest successes; she either gets discouraged or she swells with vanity; when success is expected, it is welcomed with simplicity; but it becomes an intoxicating triumph if one doubted obtaining it; that is the excuse of women who get carried away with their own importance and who ostentatiously display their least accomplishments. They constantly look back to see how far they have come: this curbs their drive.

They can have honorable careers with such methods, but will not accomplish great things. It should be said that many men too are only able to build mediocre careers. It is only in relation to the best of them that the woman—with very rare exceptions—seems to us still to be bringing up the rear. The reasons I have given sufficiently explain this and do not in any way compromise the future. To do great things, today's woman needs above all forgetfulness of self: but to forget oneself one must first be solidly sure that one has already found oneself. Newly arrived in the world of men, barely supported by them, the woman is still much too busy looking for herself.

There is one category of women to whom these remarks do not apply because their careers, far from harming the affirmation of their femininity, reinforce it; through artistic expression they seek to go beyond the very given they constitute: actresses, dancers and singers. For three centuries they have almost been the only ones to possess concrete independence in society, and today they still hold a privileged place in it. In the past, actresses were cursed by the Church: this excessive severity allowed them great freedom of behavior; they are often involved in seduction, and like courtesans they spend much of their days in the company of men: but as they earn their living themselves, finding the meaning of their existence in their work, they escape men's yoke. Their great advantage is that their professional successes contribute—as for males—to their sexual worth; by realizing themselves as human beings, they accomplish themselves as women: they are not torn between contradictory aspirations; on the contrary, they find in their jobs a justification for their narcissism: clothes, beauty care and charm are part of their professional duties; a woman infatuated with her image finds great satisfaction in *doing* something simply by exhibiting what she *is*; and this exhibition requires sufficient amounts of both artifice and study if it is to be, in Georgette Leblanc's[23] words, a substitute for action. A great actress will aim even higher: she will go beyond the given in the way she expresses it, she will really be an artist, a creator who gives meaning to her life by lending meaning to the world.

But these rare advantages also conceal traps: instead of integrating her narcissistic indulgence and the sexual freedom she enjoys into her artistic life, the actress often falls into self-worship or seduction; I have already spoken of these pseudoartists who seek only "to make a name for themselves" in the cinema or theater by representing capital to exploit in a man's arms; the comfort of masculine support is very tempting compared with the risks of a career and the harshness any real work involves. The desire for a feminine destiny—a husband, a home, children— and the spell of love are not always easily reconcilable with the desire to succeed. But above all, the admiration she feels for herself limits the actress's talent in many cases; she deludes herself as to the value of her mere presence to the extent that serious work seems useless to her; more than anything else, she prefers to place herself in the limelight and sacrifices the character she is interpreting to ham acting; she, like others, does not have the generosity to forget herself, which keeps her from going beyond herself: rare are the Rachels[24] or the Duses[25] who overcome this risk and who make of their person the instrument of their art instead of seeing in art a servant of their self. In her private life, though, the ham will exaggerate all her narcissistic defects: she will appear vain, touchy and a phony; she will treat the whole world as a stage.

Today the expressive arts are not the only ones open to women: many try their hand at creative activities. Woman's situation encourages her to seek salvation in literature and in art. Living on the margin of the masculine world, she does not grasp it in its universal guise but through a particular vision; for her it is not a group of implements and concepts but a source of feelings and emotions; she is interested in the qualities of things inasmuch as they are gratuitous and secret; taking on a negative attitude, one of refusal, she does not lose herself in the real: she protests against it, with words; she looks for the image of her soul in nature, she abandons herself to her reveries, she wants to reach her *being*: she is doomed to failure; she can only recover it in the realm of imagination. So as not to allow an inner life that does not *serve* any purpose to sink into nothingness, so as to assert herself against the given that she endures in revolt, so as to create a world other than the one in which she cannot succeed in reaching herself, she needs *to express herself.* Thus it is well-known that she is talkative and a scribbler; she pours out her feelings in conversations, letters and diaries.[26] If she is at all ambitious, she will be writing her memoirs, transposing her biography into a novel, breathing her feelings into poems. She enjoys vast leisure time that favors these activities.

But the very circumstances that orient the woman toward creation also constitute obstacles she will often be unable to overcome. When she decides to paint or write just to fill the emptiness of her days, paintings and essays will be treated as "ladies' work"; she will devote little time or care to them and they will be worth about as much. To compensate for the flaws in her existence, often the woman at menopause feverishly takes up the brush or pen: it is late; without serious training, she will never be more than an amateur. But even if she begins quite young, she rarely envisages art as serious work; used to idleness, never having experienced in her life the austere necessity of a discipline, she will not be capable of a steady and persevering effort, she will not compel herself to acquire a solid technique; she balks at the thankless and solitary trials and errors of work that is never exhibited, that has to be destroyed and done over again a hundred times; and as from childhood she was taught to cheat in order to please, she hopes to get by with a few ruses. This is what Marie Bashkirtseff[27] admits. "Yes, I don't take the trouble to paint. I watched myself today, *I cheat*." The woman easily *plays* at working but she does not work; believing in the magic virtues of passivity, she confuses conjurations and acts, symbolic gestures and effective behavior; she disguises herself as a Beaux-Arts student, she arms herself with her arsenal of brushes; planted in front of her easel, her gaze wanders from the blank canvas to her mirror; but the bouquet of flowers, the bowl of apples, do not appear on their own on the canvas. Seated at her desk, musing over vague stories, the woman acquires a peaceful alibi in imagining she is a writer: but she must at some point make signs on the blank page; they have to have a meaning in the eyes of others. So the trickery is exposed. To please one needs only to create mirages: but a work of art is not a mirage, it is a solid object; to construct it, one must know one's craft. It is not only thanks to her gifts or personality that Colette became a great writer; her pen was often her livelihood and she demanded of it the careful work that a good artisan demands of his tool; from *Claudine* to *Break of Day*, the amateur became professional: the progress brilliantly shows the advantages of a strict apprenticeship. Most women, though, do not understand the problems that their desire for communication poses: and this is what largely explains their laziness. They have always considered themselves as givens; they believe their worth comes from an inner grace and they do not imagine that value can be acquired; to seduce, they know only how to display themselves: their charm works or does not work, they have no grasp on its success or failure;

71

they suppose that, in a similar way, to express oneself, one needs only show what one is; instead of constituting their work by a thoughtful effort, they put their confidence in spontaneity; writing or smiling is all one to them: they try their luck, success will come or will not. Sure of themselves, they reckon that the book or painting will be successful without effort; timid, they are discouraged by the least criticism; they do not know that error can open the road to progress, they take it for an irreparable catastrophe, like a malformation. This is why they often overreact, which is harmful to themselves: they become irritated and discouraged when recognizing their errors rather than drawing valuable lessons from them. Unfortunately, spontaneity is not as simple as it appears: the paradox, of the commonplace—as Paulhan explains in *The Flowers of Tarbes*[28]—is that it is nothing more than the immediate translation of the subjective impression. Thus, when the woman produces the image she creates without taking others into account, she thinks she is most unusual, but she is merely reinventing a banal cliché; if she is told, she is surprised and vexed and throws down her pen; she is not aware that the public reads with its own eyes and its own mind and that a brand-new epithet can awaken in it many old memories; of course, it is a precious gift to be able to dig down into oneself and bring up vibrant impressions to the surface of language; one admires Colette for a spontaneity not found in any male writer; but—although these two terms seem to contradict each other—hers is a thoughtful spontaneity: she refuses some of its contributions and accepts others as she sees fit; the amateur, rather than seizing words as an interindividual relation, an appeal to the other, sees in them the direct revelation of her feelings; editing or crossing out for her means repudiating a part of self; she does not want to sacrifice anything both because she delights in what she *is* and because she hopes not to become other. Her sterile vanity comes from the fact that she cherishes herself without daring to construct herself.

Thus, very few of the legions of women who attempt to dabble in literature and art persevere; those who overcome this first obstacle very often remain divided between their narcissism and an inferiority complex. Not being able to forget oneself is a failure that will weigh on them more heavily than in any other career; if their essential goal is an abstract self-affirmation, the formal satisfaction of success, they will not abandon themselves to the contemplation of the world: they will be incapable of creating it anew. Marie Bashkirtseff decided to paint because she wanted to become famous; the obsession with glory comes between her and reality; she does not really like to paint: art is merely a means; it is not her ambitious and empty dreams that will reveal to her the meaning of a color or face. Instead of giving herself generously to the work she undertakes, the woman all too often considers it a simple ornament of her life; books and paintings are only an inessential intermediary allowing her to exhibit this essential reality publicly: her own person. Thus it is her person that is the main—sometimes only—subject that interests her: Mme Vigée-Lebrun[29] does not tire of putting her smiling maternity on her canvases. Even if she speaks of general themes, the woman writer will still speak of herself: one cannot read such and such theater reviews without being informed of the size and corpulence of their author, the color of her hair and the peculiarities of her personality. Of course, the self is not always detestable. Few books are as fascinating as certain confessions: but they have to be sincere and the author has to have something to confess. Instead of enriching the woman, her narcissism[30] impoverishes her; involved in nothing but self-contemplation, she eliminates herself; even the love she bestows on herself becomes stereotyped: she does not discover in her writings her authentic experience but an imaginary idol constructed from clichés. She cannot be criticized for projecting herself in her novels as Benjamin Constant and Stendhal did: but unfortunately she sees her story too often as a silly fairy tale; the young girl hides the brutal and frightening reality from herself with good doses of fantasizing: it is a pity that once she is an adult, she still buries the world, its characters, and herself in the fogginess of poetry. When the truth emerges from this travesty, there are sometimes charming successes, but next to *Dusty Answer* or *The Constant Nymph*,[31] how many bland and dull escapist novels there are!

It is natural for women to try to escape this world where they often feel unrecognized and misunderstood; what is regrettable is that they do not dare the bold flights of a Gérard de Nerval or a Poe. Many reasons excuse woman's timidity. Her great concern is to please; and as a woman she is often already afraid of displeasing just because she writes: the term "bluestocking," albeit a bit overused, still has a disagreeable connotation; she lacks the courage to displease even more as a writer. The writer who is original, as long as he is not dead, is always scandalous; what is new disturbs and antagonizes; women are still astonished and flattered to be accepted into the world of thinking and art, a masculine world: the woman watches her manners; she does not dare to irritate, explore, explode; she thinks she has to excuse her literary pretensions by her modesty and good taste; she relies on the proven values of conformism; she introduces just the personal note that is expected of her into her literature: she points out that she is a woman with some well-chosen affectations, simpering and preciosities; so she will excell at producing "bestsellers" but she cannot be counted on to blaze new trails. Women do not lack originality in their behavior and feelings: there are some so singular that they have to be locked up; on the whole, many of them are more baroque and eccentric than the men whose strictures they reject. But they put their bizarre genius into their lives, conversation and correspondence; if they try to write, they feel crushed by the universe of culture because it is a universe of men: they just babble. Inversely, the woman who chooses to reason, to express herself using masculine techniques, will do her best to stifle an originality she distrusts; like a female student, she will be assiduous and pedantic; she will imitate rigor and virile vigor. She may become an excellent theoretician and acquire a solid talent; but she will make herself repudiate everything in her that is "different." There are women who are mad and there are women of talent: none of them has this madness in talent called genius.

This reasonable modesty is what has above all defined the limits of feminine talent until now. Many women have eluded—and they increasingly elude—the traps of narcissism and faux wonderment; but no woman has ever thrown prudence to the wind to try to *emerge* beyond the given world. In the first place, there are, of course, many who accept society just as it is; they are par excellence the champions of the bourgeoisie since they represent the most conservative element of this threatened class; with well-chosen adjectives, they evoke the refinements of a civilization "of quality"; they extol the bourgeois ideal of happiness and disguise their class interests under the banner of poetry; they orchestrate the mystification intended to persuade women to "remain women"; old houses, parks and kitchen gardens, picturesque grandparents, mischievous children, laundry, jams and jellies, family gatherings, clothes, salons, balls, suffering but exemplary wives, the beauty of devotion and sacrifice, small disappointments and great joys of conjugal love, dreams of youth, mature resignation— women novelists from England, France, America, Canada and Scandinavia have exploited these themes to the utmost; they have attained glory and wealth but have not enriched our vision of the world. Far more interesting are the women insurgents who have indicted this unjust society; protest literature can give rise to strong and sincere works; George Eliot drew from her revolt a detailed and dramatic vision of Victorian England; however, as Virginia Woolf[32] shows, Jane Austen, the Brontë sisters and George Eliot had to spend so much negative energy freeing themselves from external constraints that they arrived out of breath at the point where the major masculine writers were starting out; they have little strength left to benefit from their victory and break all the ties that bind them: for example, they lack the irony, the nonchalance, of a Stendhal or his calm sincerity. Nor have they had the wealth of experience of a Dostoevsky, a Tolstoy: it is why the great book *Middlemarch* does not equal *War and Peace*; *Wuthering Heights*,[33] in spite of its stature, does not have the scope of *The Brothers Karamazov*. Today, women already have less trouble asserting themselves; but they have not totally overcome the age-old specification that confines them in their femininity. Lucidity, for example, is a conquest they are justly proud of but with which they are a little too quickly satisfied. The fact is that the traditional woman is a mystified consciousness and an instrument of mystification; she tries to conceal her dependence from herself, which is a way of consenting to it; to denounce this dependence is already a liberation; cynicism is a defense against humiliation and shame: it is the first stage of assuming responsibility. In trying to be lucid, women writers render the greatest service to the cause of women; but—without generally realizing it—they remain too attached to serving this cause to adopt, in front of the whole world, the disinterested attitude that opens up wider horizons. When they pull away the veils of illusion and lies, they think they have done enough: nonetheless, this negative daring still leaves us with an enigma; for truth itself is ambiguity, depth, mystery: after its presence is acknowledged, it must be thought, re-created. It is all well and good not to be duped: but this is where it all begins; the woman exhausts her courage in dissipating mirages and she stops in fear at the threshold of reality. This is why, for example, there are sincere and endearing women's autobiographies: but none can compare with *Confessions* or *Memoirs of an Egotist*.[34] We women are still too preoccupied with seeing clearly to try to penetrate other shadows beyond that clarity.

"Women never go beyond the pretext," a writer told me. This is true enough. Still amazed at having had permission to explore the world, they take its inventory without trying to discover its meaning. Where they sometimes excel is in the observation of facts: they make remarkable reporters; no male journalist has outdone Andrée Viollis's[35] eyewitness reports on Indochina and India. They know how to describe atmosphere and people, to show the subtle relations between them, and let us share in the secret workings of their souls: Willa Cather,[36] Edith Wharton,[37] Dorothy Parker and Katherine Mansfield[38] have sharply and sensitively brought to life individuals, climates and civilizations. They have rarely succeeded in creating as convincing a masculine hero as Heathcliff:[39] they grasp little more than the male in man; but they often describe their own interior lives, experiences and universe very well; attached to the secret side of objects, fascinated by the uniqueness of their own sensations, they convey their fresh experience through the use of savory adjectives and sensual images; their vocabulary is usually more noticeable than their syntax because they are interested in things more than their relations; they do not aim for abstract elegance; instead, their words speak to the senses. One area they have most lovingly explored is Nature; for the girl or the woman who has not completely abdicated, nature represents what woman represents for man: herself and her negation, a kingdom and a place of exile; she is all in the guise of the other. The woman writer will most intimately reveal her experience and dreams in speaking of moors or kitchen gardens. There are many who enclose the miracles of sap and seasons in pots, vases and flower beds; others, without imprisoning plants and animals, nonetheless try to appropriate them by the attentive love they dispense to them: so it is with Colette and Katherine Mansfield;

very rare are those who approach nature in its inhuman freedom, who try to decipher its foreign meanings and lose themselves in order to unite with this other presence: hardly any women venture down these roads Rousseau invented, except for Emily Brontë, Virginia Woolf and sometimes Mary Webb.[40] And to an even greater extent we can count on the fingers of one hand the women who have traversed the given in search of its secret dimension: Emily Brontë explored death, Virginia Woolf life, and Katherine Mansfield sometimes—not very often—daily contingence and suffering. No woman ever wrote *The Trial*, *Moby-Dick*, *Ulysses*, or *The Seven Pillars of Wisdom*.[41] Women do not challenge the human condition because they have barely begun to be able to assume it entirely. This explains why their works generally lack metaphysical resonance and black humor as well; they do not set the world apart, they do not question it, they do not denounce its contradictions: they take it seriously. The fact is that most men have the same limitations as well; it is when she is compared with the few rare artists who deserve to be called "great" that woman comes out as mediocre. Destiny is not what limits her: it is easy to understand why it has not been possible for her to reach the highest summits, and why it will perhaps not be possible for some time.

Art, literature and philosophy are attempts to found the world anew on a human freedom: that of the creator; to foster such an aim, one must first unequivocally posit oneself as a freedom. The restrictions that education and custom impose on woman limit her grasp of the universe; when the struggle to claim a place in this world gets too rough, there can be no question of tearing oneself away from it; one must first emerge within it in sovereign solitude if one wants to try to grasp it anew: what woman primarily lacks is learning from the practice of abandonment and transcendence, in anguish and pride. Marie Bashkirtseff writes:

What I want is the freedom to walk around alone, come and go, sit on park benches in the Tuileries Gardens. Without this freedom you cannot become a true artist. You think you can profit from what you see when you are being accompanied or when you must wait for your car, your nursemaid, your family to go to the Louvre! . . . This is the freedom that is missing and without which one cannot seriously become something. *Thinking is imprisoned by this stupid and incessant constraint . . . That is all it takes to clip one's wings.* This is one of the reasons there are no women artists.

Indeed, for one to become a creator, it is not enough to be cultivated, that is, to make going to shows and meeting people part of one's life; culture must be apprehended through the free movement of a transcendence; the spirit with all its riches must project itself in an empty sky that is its to fill; but if a thousand fine bonds tie it to the earth, its surge is broken. The girl today can certainly go out alone, stroll in the Tuileries; but I have already said how hostile the street is: eyes everywhere, hands waiting; if she wanders absentmindedly, her thoughts elsewhere, if she lights a cigarette in a café, if she goes to the cinema alone, an unpleasant incident can quickly occur; she must inspire respect by the way she dresses and behaves: this concern rivets her to the ground and to self. "Her wings are clipped." At eighteen, T. E. Lawrence[42] went on a grand tour through France by bicycle; a young girl would never be permitted to take on such an adventure: still less would it be possible for her to take off on foot for a half-desert and dangerous country as Lawrence did. Yet, such experiences have an inestimable impact: this is how an individual in the headiness of freedom and discovery learns to look at the entire world as his fief. The woman is already naturally deprived of the lessons of violence: I have said how physical weakness disposes her to passivity; when a boy settles a fight with punches, he feels he can rely on himself in his own interest; at least the girl should be allowed to compensate by sports, adventure and the pride of obstacles overcome. But no. She may feel alone *within* the world: she never stands up *in front* of it, unique and sovereign. Everything encourages her to be invested and dominated by foreign existences: and particularly in love, she disavows rather than asserts herself. Misfortune and distress are often learning experiences in this sense: it was isolation that enabled Emily Brontë to write a powerful and unbridled book; in the face of nature, death and destiny, she relied on no one's help but her own. Rosa Luxemburg[43] was ugly; she was never tempted to wallow in the cult of her image, to make herself object, prey and trap: from her youth she was wholly mind and freedom. Even then, it is rare for a woman to fully assume the agonizing tête-à-tête with the given world. The constraints that surround her and the whole tradition that weighs on her keep her from feeling responsible for the universe: this is the profound reason for her mediocrity.

Men we call great are those who—in one way or another—take the weight of the world on their shoulders; they have done more or less well, they have succeeded in re-creating it or they have failed; but they took on this enormous burden in the first place. This is what no woman has ever done, what no woman has ever been *able* to do. It takes belonging to the privileged caste to view the universe as one's own, to consider oneself as guilty of its faults and take pride in its progress; those alone who are at the controls have the opportunity to justify it by changing, thinking and revealing it; only they can identify with it and try to leave their imprint on it. Until now it has only been possible for Man to be incarnated in the man, not the woman. Moreover, individuals who appear exceptional to us, the ones we honor with the name of genius, are those who tried to work out the fate of all humanity in their particular lives. No woman has thought herself authorized to do that. How could van Gogh have

83

been born woman? A woman would not have been sent on a mission to Borinage, she would not have felt men's misery as her own crime, she would not have sought redemption; so she would never have painted van Gogh's sunflowers. And this is without taking into account that the painter's kind of life—the solitude in Arles, going to cafés, whorehouses, everything that fed into van Gogh's art by feeding his sensibility— would have been prohibited to her. A woman could never have become Kafka: in her doubts and anxieties, she would never have recognized the anguish of Man driven from paradise. St. Teresa is one of the only women to have lived the human condition for herself, in total abandonment: we have seen why.[44] Placing herself beyond earthly hierarchies, she, like St. John of the Cross, felt no reassuring sky over her head. For both of them it was the same night, the same flashes of light, in each the same nothingness, in God the same plenitude. When finally it is possible for every human being to place his pride above sexual differences in the difficult glory of his free existence, only then will woman be able to make her history, her problems, her doubts and her hopes those of humanity; only then will she be able to attempt to discover in her life and her works all of reality and not only her own person. As long as she still has to fight to become a human being, she cannot be a creator.

Once again, to explain her limits, we must refer to her situation and not to a mysterious essence: the future remains wide open. The idea that woman has no "creative genius" has been defended ad nauseam; Mme Marthe Borély,[45] a noted antifeminist of former times, defends this thesis, among others: but it looks as if she tried to make her books the living proof of incoherence and feminine silliness, and so they contradict themselves. Besides, the idea of a given creative "instinct" must be rejected like that of the "eternal feminine" and put away in the attic of entities. Some misogynists affirm a bit more concretely that because women are neurotic, they will never create anything of value: but these same people often declare that genius is a neurosis. In any case, the example of Proust shows clearly enough that psychophysiological imbalance does not mean powerlessness or mediocrity. As for the argument drawn from history, we have just seen what we should think of it; the historical past cannot be considered as defining an eternal truth; it merely translates a situation that is showing itself to be historical precisely in that it is in the process of changing. How could women ever have had genius when all possibility of accomplishing a work of genius—or just a work— was refused them? Old Europe formerly heaped its contempt on barbarian Americans for possessing neither artists nor writers: "Let us live before asking us to justify our existence," Jefferson[46] wrote, in essence. Blacks give the same answers to racists who reproach them for not having produced a Whitman or Melville. Neither can the French proletariat invoke a name like Racine or Mallarmé. The free woman is just being born; when she conquers herself, she will perhaps justify Rimbaud's prophecy: "Poets will be. When woman's infinite servitude is broken, when she lives for herself and by herself, man—abominable until now—giving her her freedom, she too will be a poet! Woman will find the unknown! Will her worlds of ideas differ from ours? She will find strange, unfathomable, repugnant, delicious things, we will take them, we will understand them."[*47] Her "worlds of ideas" are not necessarily different from men's, because she will free herself by assimilating them; to know how singular she will remain and how important these singularities will continue to be, one would have to make some foolhardy predictions. What is beyond doubt is that until now women's possibilities have been stifled and lost to humanity, and in her and everyone's interest it is high time she be left to take her own chances.

---

* Rimbaud to Paul Demeny, May 15, 1871.

CONCLUSION

"No, woman is not our brother; through negligence and corruption, we have made her a being apart, unknown, having no weapon but her sex, which is not only perpetual war but in addition an unfair weapon—adoring or hating, but not a frank companion or a being with *esprit de corps* and freemasonry—of the eternal little slave's defiances."

Many men would still subscribe to these words of Jules Laforgue;[1] many think that there will always be Sturm und Drang between the two sexes and that fraternity will never be possible for them. The fact is that neither men nor women are satisfied with each other today. But the question is whether it is an original curse that condemns them to tear each other apart or whether the conflicts that pit them against each other express a transitory moment in human history.

We have seen that in spite of legends, no physiological destiny imposes eternal hostility on the Male and Female as such; even the notorious praying mantis devours her male only for lack of other food and for the good of the species: in the animal kingdom, from the top of the ladder to the bottom, all individuals are subordinated to the species. Moreover, humanity is something other than a species: it is an historical becoming; it is defined by the way it assumes natural facticity. Indeed, even with the greatest bad faith in the world, it is impossible to detect a rivalry between the male and the female human that is specifically physiological. And so their hostility is located on that ground that is intermediate between biology and psychology, namely, psychoanalysis. Woman, it is said, envies man's penis and desires to castrate him, but the infantile desire for the penis only has importance in the adult woman's life if she experiences her femininity as a mutilation; and it is only to the extent that the penis embodies all the privileges of virility that she wishes to appropriate the male organ for herself. It is generally agreed that her dream of castration has a symbolic significance: she wishes, so it is thought, to deprive the male of his transcendence. Her wish, as we have seen, is much more ambiguous: she wishes, in a contradictory way, *to have* this transcendence, which presupposes that she both respects and denies it, and that she intends both to throw herself into it and to keep it within herself. This means that the drama does not unfold on a sexual level; sexuality, moreover, has never seemed to us to define a destiny or to provide in itself the key to human behavior, but to express the totality of a situation it helps define. The battle of the sexes is not immediately implied by the anatomy of man and woman. In fact, when it is mentioned, it is taken for granted that in the timeless heaven of Ideas a battle rages between these uncertain essences: the Eternal Feminine and the Eternal Masculine; and it is not noticed that this titanic combat assumes two totally different forms on earth, corresponding to different historical moments.

The woman confined to immanence tries to keep man in this prison as well; thus the prison will merge with the world and she will no longer suffer from being shut up in it: the mother, the wife, the lover are the jailers; society codified by men decrees that woman is inferior: she can only abolish this inferiority by destroying male superiority. She does her utmost to mutilate, to dominate man, she contradicts him, she denies his truth and values. But in doing that, she is only defending herself; neither immutable essence nor flawed choice has doomed her to immanence and inferiority. They were imposed on her. All oppression creates a state of war. This particular case is no exception. The existent considered as inessential cannot fail to attempt to reestablish his sovereignty.

Today, the combat is taking another form; instead of wanting to put man in prison, woman is trying to escape from it; she no longer seeks to drag him into the realms of immanence but to emerge into the light of transcendence. And the male attitude here creates a new conflict: the man petulantly "dumps" the woman. He is pleased to remain the sovereign subject, the absolute superior, the essential being; he refuses to consider his companion concretely as an equal; she responds to his defiance by an aggressive attitude. It is no longer a war between individuals imprisoned in their respective spheres: a caste claiming its rights lays siege but is held in check by the privileged caste. Two transcendences confront each other; instead of mutually recognizing each other, each freedom wants to dominate the other.

This difference in attitude is manifest on the sexual as well as the spiritual level; the "feminine" woman, by becoming a passive prey, tries to reduce the male to carnal passivity as well; she works at entrapping him, at imprisoning him, by the desire she arouses, docilely making herself a thing; the "emancipated" woman, on the contrary, wants to be active and prehensile and refuses the passivity the man attempts to impose on her. Likewise, Élise and her followers do not accord any value to virile activities; they place flesh above spirit, contingence above freedom, conventional wisdom above creative daring. But the "modern" woman accepts masculine values: she prides herself on thinking, acting, working and creating on the same basis as males; instead of trying to belittle them, she declares herself their equal.

This claim is legitimate insofar as it is expressed in concrete ways; and it is men's insolence that is then reprehensible. But in their defense it must be said that women themselves tend to confuse the issue. A Mabel Dodge[2] attempted to enslave Lawrence by her feminine wiles in order to then dominate him spiritually; to show by their successes that they equal a man, many women strive to secure masculine support

90

through sex; they play both sides, demanding both old-fashioned respect and modern esteem, relying on their old magic and their fledgling rights; it is understandable that the irritated man should go on the defensive, but he too is duplicitous when he demands that the woman play the game loyally whereas he, in his hostility and distrust, refuses to grant her indispensable trump cards. In reality, the struggle between them cannot be clear-cut, since woman's very being is opacity; she does not stand in front of man as a subject but as an object paradoxically endowed with subjectivity; she assumes herself as both *self* and *other*, which is a contradiction with disconcerting consequences. When she makes a weapon of both her weakness and her strength, it is not a deliberate calculation: she is spontaneously seeking her salvation in the path imposed on her, that of passivity, at the same time as she is actively demanding her sovereignty; and this process is undoubtedly not "fair play," but it is dictated by the ambiguous situation assigned to her. Man, though, when he treats her like a freedom, is indignant that she is still a trap for him; while he flatters and satisfies her in her role as his prey, he gets annoyed at her claims to autonomy; whatever he does, he feels duped and she feels wronged.

The conflict will last as long as men and women do not recognize each other as peers, that is, as long as femininity is perpetuated as such; which of them is the most determined to maintain it? The woman who frees herself from it nevertheless wants to conserve its prerogatives; and the man then demands that she assume its limitations. "It is easier to accuse one sex than to excuse the other," says Montaigne. Meting out blame and approbation is useless. In fact, the vicious circle is so difficult to break here because each sex is victim both of the other and of itself; between two adversaries confronting each other in their pure freedom, an agreement could easily be found, especially as this war does not benefit anyone; but the complexity of this whole business comes from the fact that each camp is its enemy's accomplice; the woman pursues a dream of resignation, the man a dream of alienation; inauthenticity does not pay: each one blames the other for the unhappiness brought on himself by taking the easy way out; what the man and the woman hate in each other is the striking failure of their own bad faith or their own cowardice.

We have seen why men originally enslaved women;[3] the devaluation of femininity was a necessary step in human development; but this step could have brought about a collaboration between the two sexes; oppression is explained by the tendency of the existent to flee from himself by alienating himself in the other that he oppresses for that purpose; this tendency can be found in each individual man today: and the vast majority give in to it; a husband looks for himself in his wife, a lover in his mistress, in the guise of a stone statue; he seeks in her the myth of his virility, sovereignty, his unmediated reality. "My husband never goes to the movies," says the woman, and the dubious masculine pronouncement is engraved in the marble of eternity. But he himself is a slave to his double: what effort to build up an image in which he is always in danger! After all, it is founded on the capricious freedom of women: it must constantly be made favorable; man is consumed by the concern to appear male, important, superior; he playacts so that others will playact with him; he is also aggressive and nervous; he feels hostility for women because he is afraid of them, and he is afraid of them because he is afraid of the character with whom he is assimilated. What time and energy he wastes in getting rid of, idealizing and transposing complexes, in speaking about women, seducing and fearing them! He would be liberated with their liberation. But that is exactly what he fears. And he persists in the mystifications meant to maintain woman in her chains.

That she is mystified is something of which many men are conscious. "What a curse to be a woman! And yet the very worst curse when one is a woman is, in fact, not to understand that it is one, says Kierkegaard."[4] Attempts have been made to disguise this

* _In Vino Veritas_. He also says: "Gallantry is essentially woman's due; and the fact that she unconsciously accepts it may be explained by the solicitude of nature for the weak and the disadvantaged, those who feel more than recompensed by an illusion. But this illusion is precisely fatal . . . Is it not an even worse mockery to feel freed from misery—thanks to one's imagination, to be the dupe of imagination? Woman certainly is far from being _verwahrlost_ [abandoned]; but inasmuch as she never can free herself from the illusion with which nature consoles her, she is."

misfortune for a long time. Guardianship, for example, was eliminated: the woman was given "protectors" and if they were endowed with the rights of the old guardians, it was in her best interest. Forbidding her to work and keeping her at home is intended to defend her against herself and ensure her happiness. We have seen the poetic veils used to hide the monotonous burdens she bears: housework and maternity; in exchange for her freedom she was given fallacious treasures of "femininity" as a gift. Balzac described this maneuver very well in advising a man to treat her as a slave while persuading her she is a queen. Less cynical, many men endeavor to convince themselves she is truly privileged. There are American sociologists seriously teaching today the theory of "low-class gain," that is, the "advantages of the lower castes." In France as well it has often been proclaimed—albeit less scientifically—that workers are indeed lucky not to be obliged to "present well," and, even more so tramps who could dress in rags and sleep on the streets, pleasures that were forbidden to the conte de Beaumont and those poor Wendel[5] gentlemen. Like the filthy carefree souls cheerfully scratching their vermin, like the joyful Negroes laughing while being lashed, and like these gay Arabs of Sousse with a smile on their lips, burying their children who starved to death, the woman enjoys this incomparable privilege: irresponsibility. Without difficulties, without responsibility, without cares, she obviously has "the best part." What is troubling is that by a stubborn perversity—

undoubtedly linked to original sin—across centuries and countries, the people who have the best part always shout to their benefactors: It's too much! I'll settle for yours! But the magnanimous capitalists, the generous colonialists, the superb males persist: Keep the best part, keep it!

The fact is that men encounter more complicity in their woman companions than the oppressor usually finds in the oppressed; and in bad faith they use it as a pretext to declare that woman *wanted* the destiny they imposed on her. We have seen that in reality her whole education conspires to bar her from paths of revolt and adventure; all of society—beginning with her respected parents—lies to her in extolling the high value of love, devotion and the gift of self and in concealing the fact that neither lover, husband nor children will be disposed to bear the burdensome responsibility of it. She cheerfully accepts these lies because they invite her to take the easy slope: and that is the worst of the crimes committed against her; from her childhood and throughout her life, she is spoiled, she is corrupted by the fact that this resignation, tempting to any existent anxious about her freedom, is meant to be her vocation; if one encourages a child to be lazy by entertaining him all day, without giving him the occasion to study, without showing him its value, no one will say when he reaches the age of man that he chose to be incapable and ignorant; this is how the woman is raised, without ever being taught the necessity of assuming her own existence; she readily lets herself count on the protection, love, help and guidance of others; she lets herself be fascinated by the hope of being able to realize her being without doing anything. She is wrong to yield to this temptation; but the man is ill-advised to reproach her for it since it is he himself who tempted her. When a conflict breaks out between them, each one will blame the other for the situation; she will blame him for creating it: no one taught me to reason, to earn my living . . . He will blame her for accepting it: you know nothing, you are incompetent . . . Each sex thinks it can justify itself by taking the offensive: but the wrongs of one do not absolve the other.

The innumerable conflicts that set men and women against each other stem from the fact that neither sex assumes all the consequences of this situation that one proposes and the other undergoes: this problematic notion of "equality in inequality" that one uses to hide his despotism and the other her cowardice does not withstand the test of experience: in their exchanges, woman counts on the abstract equality she was guaranteed, and man the concrete inequality he observes. From there ensues the endless debate on the ambiguity of the words "give" and "take" in all relationships: she complains of giving everything; he protests that she takes everything from him. The woman has to understand that an exchange—a basic law of political economy—is negotiated according to the value the proposed merchandise has for the buyer and not for the seller: she was duped by being persuaded she was priceless; in reality she is merely a distraction, a pleasure, company, an inessential article for the man; for her he is the meaning, the justification of her existence; the two objects exchanged are thus not of the same quality; this inequality will be particularly noticeable because the time they spend together—and that fallaciously seems to be the same time—does not have the same value for both partners; during the evening the lover spends with his mistress, he might be doing something useful for his career, seeing friends, cultivating relations, entertaining himself; for a man normally integrated into his society, time is a positive asset: money, reputation, pleasure. By contrast, for the idle and bored woman time is a burden she aspires to get rid of; she considers it a benefit to succeed in killing time: the man's presence is pure profit, in many cases, what interests man the most in a relationship is the sexual gain he draws from it: he can, at worst, settle for spending just enough time with his mistress to perform the sex act, but what she herself wants—with rare exceptions—is to "dispose of" all this excess time she has on her hands: and—like the shopkeeper who will not sell his potatoes if one does not "take" his turnips—she only gives her body if the lover "takes" hours of conversation and outings into the bargain. Balance can be established if the cost of the whole matter does not seem too high to the man: that depends, of course, on how intense is his desire and how important to him the occupations he sacrifices; but if the woman demands—offers—too much

97

time, she becomes completely importunate, like the river that overflows its banks, and the man will choose to have nothing rather than to have too much. So she moderates her demands; but very often a balance is found at the price of a twofold tension: she believes that the man *has* her at a bargain price; he thinks he is paying too much. Of course this explanation is somewhat humorous; but—except in cases of jealous and exclusive passion where the man wants the woman in her entirety—this conflict, in tenderness, desire, even love, is always present; the man always has "something else to do" with his time, whereas she is trying to get rid of hers; and he does not consider the hours she devotes to him as a gift but as a burden. Generally, he consents to tolerate it because he knows he is on the privileged side, he has a "guilty conscience"; and if he has any goodwill, he tries to compensate for the unequal conditions with generosity; however, he gives himself credit for being compassionate and at the first clash he treats the woman as ungrateful, he gets irritated: I am too generous. She feels she is acting like a beggar while she is convinced of the high value of her gifts, and this humiliates her. This explains the cruelty of which the woman often shows herself capable; she feels "self-righteous" because she has the bad role; she does not feel any obligation to accommodate the privileged caste, she thinks only of defending herself; she will even be very happy if she has the opportunity to display her resentment to the lover who has not been able to satisfy her: since he does not give enough, she will take everything back with fierce pleasure. Then the wounded man discovers the total price of the relationship whose every minute he disdained: he agrees to all the promises, even if it means he will again consider himself exploited when he has to honor them; he accuses his mistress of blackmailing him: she blames him for his stinginess; both consider themselves frustrated. Here too it is useless to allocate excuses and criticism: justice can never be created within injustice. It is impossible for a colonial administrator to conduct himself well with the indigenous population, or a general with his soldiers; the only solution is to be neither colonialist nor military leader; but a man cannot prevent himself from being a man. So here he is, thus guilty in spite of himself and oppressed by this fault that he has not committed himself; likewise she is a victim and a shrew in spite of herself; sometimes he revolts, he chooses cruelty, but then he makes himself an accomplice of injustice, and the fault really becomes his; sometimes he allows himself to be destroyed, devoured, by his protesting victim: but then he feels duped; often he settles for a compromise that both diminishes him and puts him ill at ease. A man of goodwill will be more torn by the situation than the woman herself: in one sense, one is always better off being on the side of the defeated; but if she is also of goodwill, unable to be self-sufficient, unwilling to crush the man with the weight of her destiny, she struggles with herself in an inextricable confusion. One meets so many of these cases in daily life for which there are no satisfactory solutions because they are defined by unsatisfactory conditions: a man who sees himself as obligated to maintain a woman he no longer loves materially and morally feels he is a victim; but if he abandoned without resources the one who has committed her whole life to him, she would be a victim in an equally unjust manner. The wrong does not come from individual perversity—and bad faith arises when each person attacks the other—it comes from a situation in the face of which all individual behavior is powerless. Women are "clingy," they are a burden and they suffer from it; their lot is that of a parasite that sucks the life from a foreign organism; were they endowed with an autonomous organism, were they able to fight against the world and wrest their subsistence from it, their dependence would be abolished: the man's also. Both would undoubtedly be much better off for it.

A world where men and women would be equal is easy to imagine because it is exactly the one the Soviet revolution *promised*: women raised and educated exactly like men would work under the same conditions* and for the same salaries; erotic freedom would be accepted by custom, but the sexual act would no longer be considered a remunerable "service";

* That some arduous professions are prohibited to them does not contradict this idea: even men are seeking professional training more and more; their physical and intellectual capacities limit their choices; in any case, what is demanded is that no boundaries of sex or caste be drawn.

women would be *obliged* to provide another livelihood for themselves; marriage would be based on a free engagement that the spouses could break when they wanted to; motherhood would be freely chosen—that is, birth control and abortion would be allowed—and in return all mothers and their children would be given the same rights; maternity leave would be paid for by the society that would have responsibility for the children, which does not mean that they would be *taken* from their parents but that they would not be *abandoned* to them.

But is it enough to change laws, institutions, customs, public opinion and the whole social context for men and women to really become peers? "Women will always be women," say the skeptics; other seers prophesy that in shedding their femininity, they will not succeed in changing into men and will become monsters. This would mean that today's woman is nature's creation; it must be repeated again that within the human collectivity nothing is natural, and woman, among others, is a product developed by civilization; the intervention of others in her destiny is originary: if this process were driven in another way, it would produce a very different result. Woman is defined neither by her hormones nor by mysterious instincts but by the way she grasps, through foreign consciousnesses, her body and her relation to the world; the abyss that separates adolescent girls from adolescent boys was purposely dug out from early infancy; later, it would be impossible to keep woman from being what she *was made*, and she will always trail this past behind her; if the weight of this past is accurately measured, it is obvious that her destiny is not fixed in eternity. One must certainly not think that modifying her economic situation is enough to transform woman: this factor has been and remains the primordial factor of her development, but until it brings about the moral, social and cultural consequences it heralds and requires, the new woman cannot appear; as of now, these consequences have been realized nowhere: in the USSR no more than in France or the United States; and this is why today's woman is torn between the past and the present; most often, she appears as a "real woman" disguised as a man, and she feels as awkward in her woman's body as in her masculine garb. She has to shed her old skin and cut her own clothes. She will only be able to do this if there is a collective change. No one teacher can today shape a "female human being" that would be an exact homologue to the "male human being": if raised like a boy, the girl feels she is an exception and that subjects her to a new kind of specification. Stendhal understood this, saying: "The forest must be planted all at once." But if we suppose, by contrast, a society where sexual equality is concretely realized, this equality would newly assert itself in each individual.

If, from the earliest age, the little girl were raised with the same demands and honors, the same severity and freedom, as her brothers, taking part in the same studies and games, promised the same future, surrounded by women and men who are unambiguously equal to her, the meanings of the "castration complex" and the "Oedipus complex" would be profoundly modified. The mother would enjoy the same lasting prestige as the father if she assumed equal material and moral responsibility for the couple; the child would feel an androgynous world around her and not a masculine world; were she more affectively attracted to her father—which is not even certain—her love for him would be nuanced by a will to emulate him and not a feeling of weakness: she would not turn to passivity; if she were allowed to prove her worth in work and sports, actively rivaling boys, the absence of a penis—compensated for by the promise of a child—would not suffice to cause an "inferiority complex"; correlatively, the boy would not have a natural "superiority complex" if it were not instilled in him and if he held women in the same esteem as men.* The little girl would not seek sterile compensations in narcissism and dreams, she would not take herself as given, she would be interested in what she does, she would throw herself into her pursuits. I have said how much easier puberty would be if she surpassed it, like the boy, toward a free adult future; menstruation horrifies her only because it signifies a

* I know a little boy of eight who lives with a mother, aunt and grandmother, all three independent and active, and a grandfather who is half-senile. He has a crushing inferiority complex in relation to the female sex, though his mother tries to combat it. In his lycée he scorns his friends and professors because they are poor males.

103

brutal descent into femininity; she would also assume her youthful eroticism more peacefully if she did not feel a frightening disgust for the rest of her destiny; a coherent sexual education would greatly help her to surmount this crisis. And thanks to coeducation, the august mystery of Man would have no occasion to arise: it would be killed by everyday familiarity and open competition. Objections to this system always imply respect for sexual taboos; but it is useless to try to inhibit curiosity and pleasure in children; this only results in creating repression, obsessions and neuroses; exalted sentimentality, homosexual fervor and the platonic passions of adolescent girls along with the whole procession of nonsense and dissipation are far more harmful than a few childish games and actual experiences. What would really be profitable for the girl is that, not seeking in the male a demigod—but only a pal, a friend, a partner—she not be diverted from assuming her own existence; eroticism and love would be a free surpassing and not a resignation; she could experience them in a relationship of equal to equal. Of course, there is no question of writing off all the difficulties a child must overcome to become an adult; the most intelligent, tolerant education could not free her from having her own experiences at her own expense; what one would want is that obstacles should not accumulate gratuitously on her path. It is already an improvement that "depraved" little girls are no longer cauterized with red-hot irons; psychoanalysis has enlightened parents somewhat; yet the conditions in which woman's sexual education and initiation take place today are so deplorable that none of the objections to the idea of a radical change are valid. It is not a question of abolishing the contingencies and miseries of the human condition in her but of giving her the means to go beyond them.

Woman is the victim of no mysterious fate; the singularities that make her different derive their importance from the meaning applied to them; they can be overcome as soon as they are grasped from new perspectives; we have seen that in her erotic experience, the woman feels—and often detests—male domination: it must not be concluded that her ovaries condemn her to living on her knees eternally. Virile aggressiveness is a lordly privilege only within a system where everything conspires to affirm masculine sovereignty; and woman *feels* so deeply passive in the love act only because she already *thinks* herself that way. Many modern women who claim their dignity as human beings still grasp their sexual lives by referring back to a tradition of slavery: so it seems humiliating to them to lie under the man and be penetrated by him, and they tense up into frigidity; but if reality were different, the meaning sexual gestures and postures symbolically express would be different as well: a woman who pays, who dominates her lover, can for example feel proud of her superb inertia and think that she is enslaving the male who is actively exerting himself; and today there are already many sexually balanced couples for whom notions of victory

105

and defeat yield to an idea of exchange. In fact, man is, like woman, a flesh, thus a passivity, the plaything of his hormones and the species, uneasy prey to his desire; and she, like him, in the heart of carnal fever, is consent, voluntary gift and activity; each of them lives the strange ambiguity of existence made body in his or her own way. In these combats where they believe they are tackling each other, they are fighting their own self, projecting onto their partner the part of themselves they repudiate; instead of living the ambiguity of their condition, each one tries to make the other accept the abjection of this condition and reserves the honor of it for one's self. If, however, both assumed it with lucid modesty, as the correlate of authentic pride, they would recognize each other as peers and live the erotic drama in harmony. The fact of being a human being is infinitely more important than all the singularities that distinguish human beings; it is never the given that confers superiority: "virtue," as the Ancients called it, is defined at the level of "what depends on us." The same drama of flesh and spirit, and of finitude and transcendence, plays itself out in both sexes; both are eaten away by time, stalked by death, they have the same essential need of the other; and they can take the same glory from their freedom; if they knew how to savor it, they would no longer be tempted to contend for false privileges; and fraternity could then be born between them.

People will say that all these considerations are merely utopian because to "remake woman," society would have had to have already made her *really* man's equal; conservatives have never missed the chance to denounce this vicious circle in all analogous circumstances: yet history does not go around in circles. Without a doubt, if a caste is maintained in an inferior position, it remains inferior: but freedom can break the circle; let blacks vote and they become worthy of the vote; give woman responsibilities and she knows how to assume them; the fact is, one would not think of expecting gratuitous generosity from oppressors; but the revolt of the oppressed at times and changes in the privileged caste at other times create new situations; and this is how men, in their own interest, have been led to partially emancipate women: women need only pursue their rise and the success they obtain encourages them; it seems most certain that they will sooner or later attain perfect economic and social equality, which will bring about an inner metamorphosis.

In any case, some will object that if such a world is possible, it is not desirable. When woman is "the same" as her male, life will lose "its spice." This argument is not new either: those who have an interest in perpetuating the present always shed tears for the marvelous past about to disappear without casting a smile on the young future. It is true that by doing away with slave markets, we destroyed those great plantations lined with azaleas and camellias, we dismantled the whole delicate Southern civilization; old lace was put away in the attics of time along with the pure timbres of the Sistine castrati, and there is a certain "feminine charm" that risks turning to dust as well. I grant that only a barbarian would not appreciate rare flowers, lace, the crystal-clear voice of a eunuch or feminine charm. When shown in her splendor, the "charming woman" is a far more exalting object than "the idiotic paintings, over-doors, décors, circus backdrops, sideboards or popular illuminations" that maddened Rimbaud;[6] adorned with the most modern of artifices, worked on with the newest techniques, she comes from the remotest ages, from Thebes, Minos, Chichén Itzá; and she is also the totem planted in the heart of the African jungle; she is a helicopter and she is a bird; and here is the greatest wonder: beneath her painted hair, the rustling of leaves becomes a thought and words escape from her breasts. Men reach out their eager hands to the marvel; but as soon as they grasp it, it vanishes; the wife and the mistress speak like everyone else, with their mouths: their words are worth exactly what they are worth; their breasts as well. Does such a fleeting miracle—and one so rare— justify perpetuating a situation that is so damaging for both sexes? The beauty of flowers and women's charms can be appreciated for what they are worth; if these treasures are paid for with blood or misery, one must be willing to sacrifice them.

The fact is that this sacrifice appears particularly heavy to men; few of them really wish in their hearts to see women accomplish themselves; those who scorn woman do not see what they would have to gain, and those who cherish her see too well what they have to lose; and it is true that present-day developments not only threaten feminine charm: in deciding to live for herself, woman will abdicate the functions as double and mediator that provide her with her privileged place within the masculine universe; for the man caught between the silence of nature and the demanding presence of other freedoms, a being who is both his peer and a passive thing appears as a great treasure; he may well perceive his companion in a mythical form, but the experiences of which she is the source or pretext are no less real: and there are hardly more precious, intimate or urgent ones; it cannot be denied that feminine dependence, inferiority and misfortune give women their unique character; assuredly, women's autonomy, even if it spares men a good number of problems, will also deny them many conveniences; assuredly, there are certain ways of living the sexual adventure that will be lost in the world of tomorrow: but this does not mean that love, happiness, poetry and dreams will be banished from it. Let us beware lest our lack of imagination impoverish the future; the future is only an abstraction for us; each of us secretly laments the absence in it of what was; but tomorrow's humankind will live the future in its flesh and in its freedom; that future will be its present and humankind will in turn prefer it; new carnal and affective relations of which we cannot conceive will be born between the sexes: friendships, rivalries, complicities, chaste or sexual companionships that past centuries would not have dreamed of are already appearing. For example, nothing seems more questionable to me than a catchphrase that dooms the new world to uniformity and then to boredom. I do not see an absence of boredom in this world of ours nor that freedom has ever created uniformity First of all, certain differences between man and woman will always exist; her eroticism, and thus her sexual world, possessing a singular form, cannot fail to engender in her a sensuality, a singular sensitivity: her relation to her body, to the male body and to the child will never be the same as those man has with his body, with the female body and with the child; those who talk so much about "equality in difference" would be hard put not to grant me that there are differences in equality. Besides, it is institutions that create monotony: young and pretty, slaves of the harem are all the same in the sultan's arms; Christianity gave eroticism its flavor of sin and legend by endowing the human female with a soul; restoring woman's singular sovereignty will not remove the emotional value from amorous embraces. It is absurd to contend that orgies, vice, ecstasy and passion would become impossible if man and woman were concretely peers; the contradictions opposing flesh to spirit, instant to time, the vertigo of immanence to the appeal of transcendence, the absolute of pleasure to the nothingness of oblivion will never disappear; tension, suffering, joy and the failure and triumph of existence will always be materialized in sexuality. To emancipate woman is to refuse to enclose her in the relations she sustains with man, but not to deny them; while she posits herself for herself, she will nonetheless continue to exist for him *as well*: recognizing each other as subject, each will remain an *other* for the other; reciprocity in their relations will not do away with the miracles that the division of human beings into two separate categories engenders: desire, possession, love, dreams, adventure; and the words that move us: "to give," "to conquer," and "to unite" will keep their meaning; on the contrary, it is when the slavery of half of humanity is abolished and with it the whole hypocritical system it implies that the "division" of humanity will reveal its authentic meaning and the human couple will discover its true form.

"The direct, natural, and necessary relation of person to person is the *relation of man to woman*," said Marx.* "From the character of this relationship follows how much man as a *species-being*, as man, has come to be himself and to comprehend himself; the relation of man to woman is the most natural relation of human being to human being. It therefore reveals the extent to which man's *natural* behavior has become *human*, or the extent to which the *human* essence in him has become a *natural* essence—the extent to which his *human nature* has come to be *natural* to him."

* *Philosophical Works*, Vol. VI. Marx's italics.

This could not be better said. Within the given world, it is up to man to make the reign of freedom triumph; to carry off this supreme victory, men and women must, among other things and above and beyond their natural differentiations, unequivocally affirm their brotherhood.

NOTES

INTRODUCTION

1. *Modern Woman: The Lost Sex* by Ferdinand Lundberg and Marynia F. Farnham (New York, Harper, 1947). Dorothy Parker (1893–1967) was a famous figure in American literature at the time and was also a journalist for *Vogue*, the *New Yorker* and *Vanity Fair.*
2. According to Sylvie Le Bon, it was probably Elsa Triolet.
3. Trained as a zoologist, and founder of the famous Institute for Sex Research at Indiana University in Bloomington, Indiana, Alfred Kinsey (1894–1956) had just published *Sexual Behavior in the Human Male* (1948), immediately translated into French and generally referred to as "The Kinsey Report." *Sexual Behavior in the Human Female* was published in 1954.
4. The work (1867–1946) was published in 1946. Julien Benda wrote a favorable review of *Le Deuxième Sexe (The Second Sex)* in the December 1949–January 1950 issue of *La Nef.*
5. Four lectures given in 1946–7 in Paris at the Collège de Philosophie, by Emmanuel Lévinas (1906–95), had just been published in book form.
6. The famous sinologist Marcel Granet (1884–1940) published *La Civilisation chinoise: la vie publique et la vie privée*

113

(1948) the previous year. Simone de Beauvoir remembered these works when she was writing *La Longue Marche (The Long March)* (1957) after her trip to China.

7. Specialist of myths and religions, Georges Dumézil (1898–1986) had just published *L'Héritage indo-européen à Rome* (1949).

8. Claude Lévi-Strauss, whom Simone de Beauvoir met when preparing the *agrégation* of philosophy, was about to publish his work with the Presses universitaires de France the same year as *Le Deuxième Sexe* (a review of the book by Simone de Beauvoir appeared in *Les Temps Modernes*, November 1949). In chapter IV of *The Force of Circumstance* she says: "Leiris tells me that Lévi-Strauss criticized me for some inaccuracies concerning primitive societies. He was finishing his thesis on *The Elementary Structures of Kinship* and I asked him to tell me about it. Several consecutive mornings I went to his house; I set myself up at a table and read a typed copy of his book; it confirmed my idea of the woman as *other*; it showed that the male remains the essential being, even in those matrilineal so-called matriarchal societies." His work was footnoted several times in the first volume of *Le Deuxième Sexe*.

9. Simone de Beauvoir appropriated Heidegger's (1889–1976) notion of primordial *Mitsein* in *Being and Time* (1927). In *The Second Sex* she developed the idea that woman is the Other of man and her status is inessential. True equality should make the woman a *subject*, just like the man; once equality is achieved, the woman will be fully engaged in time and existence, according to Heidegger's notion.

10. The Marxist philosopher August Bebel (1840–1913)

was the author of *Die Frau und der Sozialismus (Woman and Socialism)*, published in 1893.

11. François Poullain de la Barre (1647–1725) published *De l'Egalité des Sexes, discours physique et moral où l'on voit l'importance de se défaire des préjugés en 1673 (A Physical and Moral Discourse on the Equality of Both Sexes, which shows that it is important to rid oneself of prejudices, 1673)*.

12. In the third part of the first volume of *Le Deuxième Sexe*, entitled "Myths," Simone de Beauvoir devotes a chapter to the author under the title "Montherlant or the Bread of Disgust." "Montherlant," she says, "belongs to the long male tradition of adopting Pythagoras's arrogant Manichaeanism. Following Nietzsche, he considers that the Eternal Feminine was exalted only during periods of weakness and that the hero has to rise up against the Magna Mater."

13. This quote was taken from book III, chapter 5 of the *Essays*, "On poems by Virgil," which contains, among other things, some considerations on woman and marriage.

14. Simone de Beauvoir refers again to chapter 5 of book III of the *Essays*.

15. Denis Diderot made statements about women several times, in particular in a review of a work called *On Women* (1772). His opinions in this area are perhaps more contradictory than Simone de Beauvoir wants to admit.

16. The philosopher John Stuart Mill (1806–73) was the author of *The Subjection of Women*, published in 1869.

17. Simone de Beauvoir refers to the nineteenth-century debates between those fighting for women's access to civil rights (George Sand, for example) and those seeking to obtain political rights at the same time (like Flora

Tristan and the Saint-Simonians, who forcefully made their opinions heard in 1848, to no avail).

18. Laws implemented in the early twentieth century in the south of the USA to limit the rights granted to former slaves freed following the Civil War, in order to segregate schools, restaurants, hospitals, public places and means of transportation (Jim Crow was a character created for the stage by the actor Thomas Rice). School segregation was abolished in 1954, and the other forms of segregation by the 1964 Civil Rights Act.

19. The discovery of the camps at the end of the war gave this "problem" a particularly dramatic dimension (see chapter 1, *The Force of Circumstance*), leading to Sartre's *Anti-Semite and Jew* (1946).

20. Bernard Shaw (1856–1950), Irish writer and drama critic, was the author of many plays; the origin of the quote has not been found.

21. Student-edited newspaper for Latin Quarter students; some great artists and cartoonists made their debuts there.

22. Claude Mauriac (1914–96), oldest son of François Mauriac, was General de Gaulle's secretary from 1944 to 1949. A journalist at *Le Figaro*, literary critic and novelist, he was very hostile toward Sartre's philosophical and political positions, as well as toward Simone de Beauvoir's feminist analyses.

23. Michel Carrouges's article ("Les pouvoirs de la femme") in the *Cahiers du Sud* (issue 292) was also footnoted in the first volume of *Le Deuxième Sexe* (third part, "Myths," p.164 in the Vintage Classics edition). Founded in Marseille in 1925 by Jean Ballard, the *Cahiers du Sud* was a journal of reference (Sartre, notably, had published a review of *The Stranger* by Camus).

24. In the period between the two wars, it was the fight for civil rights that mobilized the feminists: they demanded the right to vote and the revision of the Civil Code.

THE INDEPENDENT WOMAN

1. General de Gaulle granted women the right to vote and to run for election in Algiers, April 21, 1944. In 1945 twelve million women went to the polls for the first time.
2. Cf. *The Second Sex*, II, third part, chapter 13.
3. The question is still topical (cf. *L'Injustice ménagère*, ed. François de Singly, Armand Colin, 2007).
4. Cf. *The Second Sex*, II, first part, chapter 4, "The Lesbian."
5. Cf. *The Second Sex*, II, first part, chapter 2, "The Girl," and *Memoirs of a Dutiful Daughter* (1958).
6. Cf. *The Second Sex*, I, first part, chapter 1, "Biological Data," and II, second part, chapter 5, "The Married Woman."
7. Fear of unwanted pregnancy was always very present, the means of contraception being rather rudimentary and abortion strictly prohibited. See notes 19 and 20 on p. xx.
8. Cf. *The Second Sex*, II, first part, chapter 2, "The Girl."
9. Colette's novel, featuring an affair between an adolescent and a mature woman, came out in 1923.
10. In his *Confessions* Jean-Jacques Rousseau recounted how he fell in love with his hostess, Mme de Warens, in 1736 and spent two very happy years with her before leaving her to go to Milan.
11. *The Little Black Book of Crisélidis* was published in 1915.
12. *The Human Condition* came out in 1933 and won the Prix Goncourt.

13. Cf. *The Second* Sex, II, third part, chapter 12, "The Woman in Love."

14. In *The Second Sex* (I, third part, chapter 2), Simone de Beauvoir devoted a section to "Stendhal or Romancing the Real."

15. Colette's novel appeared in 1910.

16. Under the name Colette Yver, Antoinette de Bergerin (married name Huzard) (1874–1953) published a number of novels as well as several romanticized biographies. "My father was not a feminist; he admired the wisdom in Colette Yver's novels in which the lawyer or the doctor ended up sacrificing her career for peace in the home" (*Memoirs of a Dutiful Daughter*, second part).

17. Translator, novelist, poet and journalist, Mary Ann Evans (1819–80), known in literary circles under the pseudonym George Eliot, was linked to the writer George Lewis until his death in 1878. In the second part of *Memoirs of a Dutiful Daughter* Simone de Beauvoir recalls reading *Mill on the Floss* and the great impression it made on her.

18. Cf. *The Second Sex*, II, second part, chapter 5, "The Married Woman."

19. Contraception method; the pill would only become available in France as of 1967.

20. Abortion was strictly forbidden, with women having recourse, if necessary, to backstreet abortionists or to an abortion abroad. In *The Prime of Life* (1960) Simone de Beauvoir makes the following observation: "No emotional fantasy made me want to become a mother. And moreover, it didn't seem compatible with the path I was taking: I knew that to become a writer I had to have a lot of time and a great deal of freedom." In 1971 she was one of the signatories of the "Manifesto of the 343,"

published in *Le Nouvel Observateur*, in which 343 well-known women in the intellectual, political and artistic areas announced that they had undergone an abortion. In 1973 she launched *Choisir, La Cause des femmes*, with Gisèle Halimi. See also *The Force of Circumstance*, chapter IV.

21. Richard Wright, American novelist born in Mississippi in 1908, described in *Native Son* (1940) and *Black Boy* (1945) the harsh conditions he suffered as a black child (extracts of these books were published in translation in *Les Temps Modernes*). He was connected to Sartre and Simone de Beauvoir and had them meet black activists during their respective stays in the United States. He was also a friend of Nelson Algren. His analyses had a decisive influence on Simone de Beauvoir. He died in Paris, where he had been living since 1947, in 1960 (see chapter XI of *The Force of Circumstance*).

22. Founded in 1794 and originally reserved for boys, the École Normale Supérieure, at 45 rue d'Ulm in the 5th *arrondissement*, had a section reserved for girls as of 1881, at first in a building of the former factory of Sèvres porcelain. "My mother was wary of Sèvres, and when I thought about it, I didn't want to be shut up there, out of Paris, with women," said Simone de Beauvoir in *Memoirs of a Dutiful Daughter* (second part).

23. Georgette Leblanc (1869–1941) was a famous opera singer and actress of theater and film, and the wife of Maurice Maeterlinck. She was also a writer, and among her books is *Souvenirs* (1931).

24. Elisabeth Rachel Félix, known as Rachel (1821–58), began a brilliant career at the Comédie Française as a tragedian, at the age of seventeen. She was one of the most famous actresses of the nineteenth century.

25. Eleonora Duse (1858–1924) was an Italian actress of international fame. She was linked with Gabriele D'Annunzio, in whose plays she performed.

26. Like many other girls of her time and milieu, Simone de Beauvoir kept a "notebook" on a regular basis, starting from her adolescence (see the third part of *Memoirs of a Dutiful Daughter*). She would go back to this form of narration and self-analysis from time to time in her multi-volumed autobiography. In *When Things of the Spirit Come First*, Chantal, one of the heroines, expresses herself in this form. The *Journal* that Simone de Beauvoir kept during the early months of the war was published in 1990.

27. Marie Bashkirtseff (1860–84), of Russian origin, died from tuberculosis very young, leaving pictorial works of exceptionally good quality and a *Journal* showing great refinement. Simone de Beauvoir was only able to read an incomplete edition, because the definitive one was still in progress.

28. Jean Paulhan (1884–1968) had published *Les Fleurs de Tarbesou la Terreur dans les lettres* in 1941. The first section of his study dealt primarily with the commonplace.

29. Among the paintings of Elisabeth Vigée-Lebrun (1755–1842) is the famous *Madame Vigée-Lebrun and her daughter* (1789).

30. Cf. *The Second Sex*, II, third part, chapter 11, "The Narcissist."

31. Simone de Beauvoir cites two English novels, *Dusty Answer* (1924) by Rosamund Lehman (1901–90) and *The Constant Nymph* (1927) by Margaret Kennedy (1896–1967), which she read as an adolescent.

32. Simone de Beauvoir takes up here the ideas that Virginia Woolf (1882–1941) developed in *A Room of One's Own* (1929).

33. *Middlemarch*, a novel by George Eliot published in 1871–2. *Wuthering Heights*, a novel by Emily Brontë (1818–48), published in 1847.

34. Simone de Beauvoir recalls the autobiographies of Rousseau and Stendhal. The *Memoirs* of Mme de Genlis (1825) and *The Story of My Life* by George Sand (1854–5), forgotten at that time, enabled her to modulate her judgment.

35. Andrée Viollis (1870–1950), journalist, historian and novelist. She was the author of *L'Inde contre les Anglais (India Against the English)* (1930).

36. Willa Cather, American novelist (1873–1947), the author of, among other works, the essay *Nebraska: The End of the First Cycle* (1923), in which she deplored the disappearance of the wild west.

37. Born in New York, Edith Wharton (1862–1937) was the author of a considerable body of fiction, including *The House of Mirth* (1905), *Ethan Frome* (1911) and *The Age of Innocence* (1920). She lived in France most of her life.

38. Kathleen Beauchamp, known in her literary life as Katherine Mansfield (1888–1923), was from New Zealand, but spent much of her life in France. She was the author of many books including *The Garden Party* (1922). "I loved Katherine Mansfield, her short stories, her *Journal* and her *Correspondance* [. . .]. I found romantic the character of the "woman alone" that weighed so heavily on her" (*The Prime of Life*, chapter III).

39. Hero of *Wuthering Heights* by Emily Brontë.

40. Mary Webb (1881–1927), English novelist, had recently won the Femina Prize for *Precious Bane* in 1924.

41. *The Trial* by Franz Kafka (1925), *Moby-Dick* by Herman Melville (1851), *Ulysses* by James Joyce (1922), *The Seven Pillars of Wisdom* by T. E. Lawrence (1926).

42. Thomas Edward Lawrence (1888–1935), novelist and specialist of the Near East. *The Seven Pillars of Wisdom* was a very successful book (Simone de Beauvoir read it during the summer of 1943, "lying in the grass, under the apple trees smelling of childhood"). His correspondence recounting his many trips was published in 1938.

43. Rosa Luxembourg (1871–1919), a great figure in the history of communism, of Polish origin, was the author of many works criticizing Karl Marx's analyses. She spent most of her life in Germany, founding with two other activists the "Spartakus" line whose goal was revolution, and contributing to the formation of the German Communist Party. She took part in the Spartacist insurrection of January 1919 in Berlin, was caught and then assassinated.

44. Cf. *The Second Sex*, II, third part, chapter 13, "The Mystic."

45. Marthe Borély (1880–1955) was the author of *Génie feminine français (French Feminine Genius)* (1917), and *L'Appel aux Françaises (The Call to French Women)* (1919), among other titles.

46. Thomas Jefferson (1743–1826), author of the *Declaration of Independence* (1776), was in favor of a "humanitarian liberalism." The quote is not identified.

47. This is a long letter written by Rimbaud at Charleville to Paul Demeny that opens with a "Parisian war song."

CONCLUSION

1. Simone de Beauvoir quotes "Sur la femme. Aphorismes et réflexions" by Jules Laforgue (1860–87). See *Oeuvres Complètes* (Paris, Société du Mercure de France, 1903), vol. 3, pp. 47–8.

2. Mabel Dodge (1879–1962) was a famous American figure in art and intellectual circles. She held a literary salon first in her Florence villa and then in her Fifth Avenue apartment in New York. D. H. Lawrence and his wife were guests in her house in Taos, New Mexico, where she received many artists. She was involved with him for a time. In *Saint Mawr (The Woman and the Beast)* (1925), Lawrence wrote a romanticized version of this period of his life. Mabel Dodge, on her side, published several volumes of memoirs. Simone de Beauvoir met Dodge when she was in the southwest of the United States.

3. Cf. *The Second Sex*, I, second part, "History."

4. Simone de Beauvoir quotes *The Diary of a Seducer* (1843) by Sören Kierkegaard (1813–55), in which the protagonist decides to seduce a girl, to have her and then immediately abandon her, in a sort of cynical and desperate celebration of a gratuitous act.

5. Simone de Beauvoir takes as examples a member of one of the oldest and richest aristocratic families of France and the dynasty of Lorraine industrialists, still owners of a major center of steel mills and blast furnaces.

6. *Une Saison en enfer*, "Alchimie du verbe" (1873).

BIOGRAPHY

Simone de Beauvoir left a considerable autobiographical oeuvre, plus many letters, published mostly after her death in 1986. Below are some dates and quotations concerning the period preceding the publication of *Le Deuxième Sexe* in 1949.

1908   Simone de Beauvoir's birth: "I was born at 4 a.m., January 9, 1908, in a room with white-lacquered furniture, giving on Boulevard Raspail. [. . .] Of my earliest years I have no more than a blurred impression: something red, black and warm. [. . .] Protected, pampered, amused by the constant newness of everything, I was a very gay little girl" (*Memoirs of a Dutiful Daughter* [*MDD*], first part). Her sister, nicknamed Poupette, was born in 1910. Financial difficulties caused the family to move a bit later to 71 rue de Rennes, to an apartment in which the two little girls had to share one bedroom.

1913   "In October 1913—I was five and a half—I was put into a school with a fetching name: the 'cours Désir.'" Simone de Beauvoir was given a Catholic and, as she discovered later, rather rudimentary education. Outside her studies, reading was "the great affair of my life," but books and magazines were strictly controlled by her mother. She spent the summer with her family in the Limousin region, near Uzerche, where her paternal grandfather had property.

1917   Arrival in the Cours Désir of Elizabeth Mabille, a "little, short-haired brunette." Soon nicknamed "Zaza," she quickly became Simone's best friend: "I couldn't conceive of anything better in the world than being myself and loving Zaza."

1921   As an adolescent, Simone de Beauvoir convinced herself little by little that her life would "lead her somewhere" and, unlike her mother, she would not be "doomed to a housewife's fate" (*MDD*, second part). "I was getting ugly, my nose got red; I had pimples on my face and neck that I picked at nervously [. . .] my shapeless dresses accentuated my clumsiness." She read more and more, but her mother still controlled what she read. After years of ardent piety, she lost her faith.

1925   Obtained her *baccalauréat* degree. "I got it with honors and these ladies [from the cours Désir], satisfied to be able to record this success on their rosters, praised me to the hilt" (ibid.). After that, she decided to prepare herself for a teaching career. She signed up at the Sorbonne and at the Institute Sainte-Marie in Neuilly, which gave girls a serious general education. "'Finally! Here I am, college student!' I joyously exclaimed" (ibid.). The more Simone de Beauvoir tried to liberate herself, the more conflicts she had with her parents. She fell in love with her cousin Jacques, who did not return her sentiments.

1928   Obtained her philosophy degree (TrN, equivalent of a BA). Preparation of the *agrégation*: "Deciding to prepare the competitive exam [. . .] I was gearing myself for the future. Every day now had meaning: carrying me toward a definitive liberation" (*MDD*, third part).

1929   In July, Simone de Beauvoir made friends with three students from the École Normale Supérieure, who were also preparing for the *agrégation*: Nizan, René Maheu (who dubbed her "Castor" ["TrN Beaver"]) and Sartre. His intellectual superiority over all his classmates was evident; his kindness, his attention to others and his desire to write were obvious. Simone de Beauvoir received her *agrégation* of philosophy; she came in second and Sartre was first. "What intoxicated me when I returned to Paris in September 1929 was first my liberty [. . .]. As soon as I opened my eyes in the morning I shook myself with joy" (*The Prime of Life* [*PL*], chapter 1). From that moment on, Simone de Beauvoir's destiny was sealed, and that of Sartre, too. "Our truth [. . .] was inscribed in eternity and the future would prove it: we were writers." Judged as "necessary love," as opposed to contingent loves, the strong feeling that linked them was subject to a renewable "lease." The death of Zaza, probably from meningitis.

1931   Assigned to a lycée in Marseille. "I fell in love. I climbed up into the rocks everywhere; I wandered

127

in all the little alleys, I sniffed the tar and the sea urchins on the Vieux-Port, I mingled with the crowds on the Canebière" (*PL*, chapter II). After his military service, Sartre was assigned to Le Havre and proposed marriage to Simone, which would have enabled them to be assigned to the same city; she refused, just as she refused any idea of motherhood: "he [Sartre] was satisfied with himself and I was satisfied with him [. . .] I never dreamed of seeing myself one day in flesh that came out of me." Strong interest in cinema, which she shared with Sartre.

1932 First try at a novel. Assigned to Rouen, where she stayed until 1936. "[. . .] because of the content of my courses, I was disapproved of by the Rouen bourgeoisie: they said I was kept by a rich senator" (*PL*, chapter III). The couple were friends with the actor Charles Dullin, as well as with Colette Audry, a Trotskyist activist who was very interested in psychoanalysis.

1933 Trip to London and then to Italy, where she discovered Rome and Venice. "[. . .] we saw Venice with that gaze never again to be had: the first [. . .]. It was also in Venice [. . .] that we saw some SS in brown shirts for the first time" (ibid.). In the autumn Sartre left for Berlin where he was appointed lecturer at the French Institute.

1936 Olga Kosakievitch, a young Russian student whom Sartre and Simone de Beauvoir had met the previous year, awakened a strong passion in Sartre: "We thought that human relations are constantly being invented, that in principle no form is better than another, no form is impossible" (*PL*, chapter IV). Nevertheless, this three-way relationship rapidly became a failure (Simone de Beauvoir used this "experience" as the subject of *She Came to Stay*). Trip to Naples and the south of Italy. "Back in Paris [. . .] we threw ourselves into the drama that completely overwhelmed our life for two and a half years: the Spanish war" (*PL*, chapter V). In the autumn Simone de Beauvoir was assigned to the Molière Lycée in Paris.

1937   In September, Sartre was assigned to the Pasteur Lycée in Paris. The lovers lived separately in rooms in the Mistral Hotel, 24 rue de Cels, in the 14th *arrondissement*: "[. . .] I had a couch, bookshelves and a very work-conducive desk [   ] Sartre lived above me. We had all the advantages of a shared life and none of the disadvantages" (ibid.).

1938   Turned in *La Primauté du spirituel (The Primacy of the Spirit)* to two publishers, both of whom turned it down. Beauvoir decided to shelve the project "with a smile" (this collection of short stories, which give voice to five women, was published by Gallimard in 1979 and in a new edition in 2006, under the title of *Anne, ou quand prime le spirituel (When Things of the Spirit Come First)*. Trip to Morocco with Sartre. After that, she took back the manuscript of *She Came to Stay*. "Of the influences I came under, the most obvious one is Hemingway's [. . .]. One of the characteristics I liked in his stories was his refusal of supposedly objective descriptions: landscapes, scenery, objects are always presented according to the hero's vision, in the perspective of the action" (ibid.).

1939   "In 1939, my existence shifted irrevocably [. . .]: History grasped me once and for all; I also committed myself totally and forever to literature" (ibid.). In September, Sartre was called up. From September 1 to July 14 of the following year Simone de Beauvoir kept a diary, from which she quotes extracts in chapter VI of *The Prime of Life*.

1940   Nizan was killed at the front in May. Sartre was taken prisoner in June and sent to Trèves. He was freed the following March.

1941   Foundation of an intellectual resistance group, "Socialism and liberty," which was dissolved a few months later.

1942   While Simone de Beauvoir continued to live in the Mistral Hotel, Sartre lived in several hotel rooms in the 6th *arrondissement*. They worked together regularly at the Café Flore. "The writers who thought like us had tacitly adopted certain rules. We wouldn't write for newspapers and magazines in the occupied zone, nor speak on Radio-Paris; we could work for papers in the free zone and for Radio-Vichy: everything depended on the meaning of the articles and programs" (ibid.).

1943   Simone de Beauvoir finished *Pyrrhus and Cinéas*, which was accepted by Gallimard. Publication of *She Came to Stay*, which was very successful, by the same publisher. The couple became friendly with

Michel Leiris and his wife, as well as with Raymond Queneau and Albert Camus. In the autumn they moved to the Louisiane Hotel on the rue de Seine.

1944 The circle of relations grew: Georges Limbour, Sylvia and Georges Bataille, Jacques Lacan and the Salacrous became friends of the Sartre-Beauvoir couple. Jean Genet was introduced into the group by Camus. Dinners at Picasso and Dora Maar's.

1945 "A devastated world. The day after the liberation, the torture chambers of the Gestapo were discovered, the mass graves were found" (*The Force of Circumstance* [*FC*], chapter 1). Simone de Beauvoir took a leave of absence from the university to be able to write; she continued to share her resources with those of Sartre. "Writing became a demanding profession for me. It guaranteed me my moral autonomy [. . .]. I saw in my books my veritable accomplishment" (ibid.). Sartre left for the United States, where he met American writers, including Richard Wright. Simone de Beauvoir met Violette Leduc, who gave her the manuscript of her autobiography. Publication of *Le Sang des autres (The Blood of Others)*: "The main theme was [. . .] the paradox of this existence experienced by me as my liberty and grasped as object by those who were near me. These intentions were not understood by the readership; the book was classified as 'a novel of resistance'" (*FC*, chapter II). Creation of a play, *Les Bouches inutiles (The Useless Mouths)*, which closed quickly.

1946   From April 30 to May 20 Simone de Beauvoir kept
        a diary of her trip to Switzerland with Sartre (she
        reproduced extracts in chapter II of *Force of Circum-*
        stance). Meeting with Boris Vian, one of the leaders
        of the "Zazou" movement. Publication of *Tous les*
        hommes sont mortels (All Men Are Mortal), envisaged
        "first of all as a long meandering around death"
        (*PL*, chapter VIII).

1947   Publication of a philosophical essay, *Pour une morale*
        de l'ambiguité (The Ethics of Ambiguity). Trip to the
        United States for a lecture tour. "American luxu-
        riance knocked me out: the streets, the show win-
        dows, the cars, the hairdos and the furs, the bars,
        the drugstores, the flow of the neons, the distances
        eaten up by plans, trains, cars, Greyhounds, the
        changing splendor of the landscapes, from the
        snows of Niagara to the burning deserts of Ari-
        zona" (*FC*, chapter III). In Chicago she met the
        writer Nelson Algren, with whom she was involved
        for four years. "He had this rare gift bestowed—
        that I would call goodness if this word hadn't been
        so mistreated."

1948   Publication of *l'Amérique au jour le jour (America*
        Day by Day). In September returned to the United
        States, where she traveled with Algren, and then
        to Mexico and Guatemala (some of the memories
        of this trip are told in chapter III of *The Force of Cir-*
        cumstance and in *The Mandarins*, published in 1954).

1949   In the spring, Nelson Algren came to Paris. "The
        first volume of *Le Deuxième Sexe* came out in June;
        the chapter on 'Sexual Initiation' appeared in

May in *Les Temps Modernes*, followed in June and July by the chapters that dealt with 'the lesbian' and 'motherhood.' The second volume came out in November by Gallimard" (*The Force of Circumstance*, id.).

SIMONE DE BEAUVOIR

THE INDEPENDENT WOMAN

Simone de Beauvoir was born in Paris in 1908. In 1929 she became the youngest person ever to obtain the *agrégation* in philosophy at the Sorbonne. After the war, she emerged as one of the leaders of the existentialist movement, working with Jean-Paul Sartre on *Les Temps Modernes*. *The Second Sex*, first published in 1949, has been translated into forty languages and become a landmark in the history of feminism. Beauvoir is the author of many other books, including the novel *The Mandarins*, which was awarded the Prix Goncourt. She died in 1986.

Translators Constance Borde and Sheila Malovany-Chevallier are both graduates of Rutgers University, New Jersey, and have lived, studied, and worked in Paris for more than forty years. They were faculty members at the Institut d'Études Politiques and jointly authored and translated numerous works on subjects ranging from grammar and politics to art and social sciences.